5 Ingredients

Mediterranean Diet Cookbook

1500 Flavorful and Healthy Recipes for Beginners to Reset Your Body and Boost Your Energy on a Budget (30 DAY MEAL PLAN)

Jessica Browne

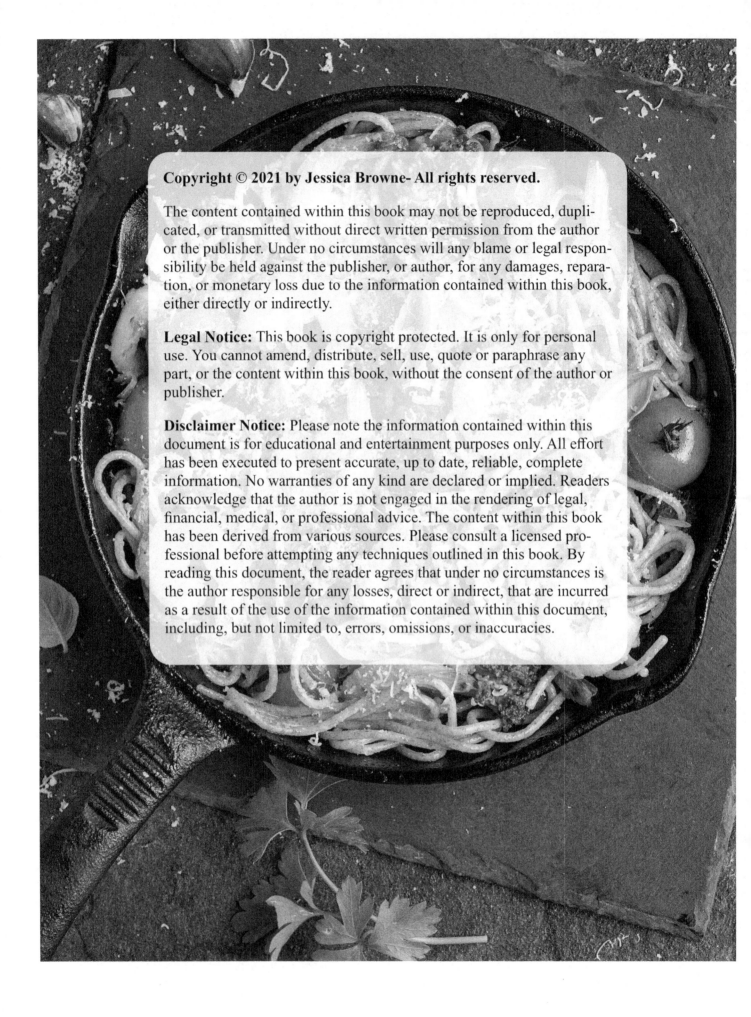

CONTENTS

Introduction 4
Get to Know Crock Pot 4

Measurement Conversions 6

Breakfast Recipes 8
Eggs Florentine With Pancetta 9
Easy Buckwheat Porridge 9
Pecan & Peach Parfait 10
Cinnamon Oatmeal With Dried Cranberries 10
Creamy Vanilla Oatmeal.................................. 11
Cheese & Mushroom Muffins 11
Avocado Toast With Goat Cheese..................... 12
Cream Peach Smoothie 12
Raspberry-yogurt Smoothie............................. 12
Mango-yogurt Smoothie 13
Chili & Cheese Frittata.................................... 13
Maple Peach Smoothie 13
One-pan Tomato-basil Eggs 14
Lime Watermelon Yogurt Smoothie 14
Maple-vanilla Yogurt With Walnuts 14
Tomato And Egg Breakfast Pizza 15
Oven-baked Mozzarella Cheese Cups.............. 15
Hot Zucchini & Egg Nests................................ 15
Easy Zucchini & Egg Stuffed Tomatoes 16
Basic Tortilla De Patatas................................. 16
Apple & Date Smoothie 16
Honey & Feta Frozen Yogurt 17
Simple Mushroom Omelet 17
Strawberry Basil Mascarpone Toast 17
5-ingredient Quinoa Breakfast Bowls 18
Berry & Cheese Omelet.................................... 18
Baked Eggs In Avocado 19
Maple Berry & Walnut Oatmeal 19
Berry-yogurt Smoothie..................................... 20
Za'atar Pizza.. 20
Anchovy & Spinach Sandwiches...................... 21
Granola & Berry Parfait 21

Beans , Grains, And Pastas Recipes 22
One-step Couscous... 23
Quinoa With Baby Potatoes And Broccoli 23
Spaghetti With Pine Nuts And Cheese 24
Swiss Chard Couscous With Feta Cheese........ 24
Cranberry And Almond Quinoa......................... 25
Parmesan Polenta.. 25
Lemon Couscous With Broccoli........................ 26
Lemon-basil Spaghetti..................................... 26
Mint Brown Rice 27
Broccoli And Carrot Pasta Salad 27
Quick Pesto Pasta 28
Raspberry & Nut Quinoa 28

Poultry And Meats Recipes 29
Easy Grilled Pork Chops 30
Peach Pork Chops.. 30
Baked Garlicky Pork Chops.............................. 31
Tomato Walnut Chicken.................................... 31
Chicken Caprese.. 31
Pork Millet With Chestnuts 32
Crispy Pesto Chicken 32
Grilled Beef With Mint-jalapeño Vinaigrette....... 33
Pork Tenderloin With Caraway Seeds 33
Rosemary Pork Loin With Green Onions 33

Original Meatballs..................................34
Greek-style Lamb Burgers.......................34

Creamy Beef Stew.................................34

Fish And Seafood Recipes 35

Parsley Tomato Tilapia 36
Dilly Haddock In Tomato Sauce.................36
Lemony Sea Bass 36
Pancetta-wrapped Scallops.....................37
Anchovy Spread With Avocado 37
Peppercorn-seared Tuna Steaks..............37
Balsamic Asparagus & Salmon Roast........38
Herby Tuna Gratin 38
Salmon Packets.....................................38
Creamy Trout Spread 39
Baked Anchovies With Chili-garlic Topping 39
Balsamic-honey Glazed Salmon 39
Grilled Lemon Pesto Salmon....................40
Salmon In Thyme Tomato Sauce 40
Glazed Broiled Salmon............................41

Rosemary Wine Poached Haddock..................41
Crunchy Pollock Fillets 42
Crab Stuffed Celery Sticks 42
Baked Salmon With Basil And Tomato 42
Simple Fried Cod Fillets 43
Instant Pot Poached Salmon........................43
Traditional Tuscan Scallops.........................44
Crispy Sole Fillets 44
Lemon-garlic Sea Bass 44
Baked Lemon Salmon 45
Baked Haddock With Rosemary Gremolata......45
Oil–poached Cod 46
Hazelnut Crusted Sea Bass 46
Parchment Orange & Dill Salmon..................47
North African Grilled Fish Fillets 47

Vegetable Mains And Meatless Recipes 48

Quick Steamed Broccoli 49
Baked Honey Acorn Squash......................49
Simple Broccoli With Yogurt Sauce 50
Garlic-butter Asparagus With Parmesan 50
Stuffed Portobello Mushrooms With Spinach....51
Tradicional Matchuba Green Beans 51
Parmesan Stuffed Zucchini Boats 52
Minty Broccoli & Walnuts 52
Roasted Asparagus With Hazelnuts................53
Baby Kale And Cabbage Salad 53

Spicy Potato Wedges 54
Sautéed Mushrooms With Garlic & Parsley 54
Garlicky Broccoli Rabe 55
Wilted Dandelion Greens With Sweet Onion.....55
Grilled Za´atar Zucchini Rounds....................56
5-ingredient Zucchini Fritters.......................56
Cauliflower Rice Risotto With Mushrooms 57
Balsamic Cherry Tomatoes...........................57
Pea & Carrot Noodles.................................58
Simple Zoodles 58

Sides , Salads, And Soups Recipes 59

Parsley Carrot & Cabbage Salad 60
Tasty Cucumber & Couscous Salad............60
Balsamic Carrots With Feta Cheese 61
Greek Chicken, Tomato, And Olive Salad 61
Green Beans With Tahini-lemon Sauce.............62
Zesty Asparagus Salad............................62
Lemony Yogurt Sauce 63
Garlic Herb Butter..................................63
Easy Roasted Cauliflower 64
Creamy Tomato Hummus Soup 64
Orange-honey Glazed Carrots 65

Herby Yogurt Sauce...................................65
Simple Tahini Sauce 66
Homemade Herbes De Provence Spice............66
Cherry, Plum, Artichoke, And Cheese Board.....66
Asparagus & Red Onion Side Dish 67
Greek Tahini Sauce 67
Roasted Cherry Tomato & Fennel 67
Balsamic Watermelon & Feta Salad................68
Arugula, Watermelon, And Feta Salad 68
Classic Potato Salad With Green Onions..........68
Quick Za´atar Spice....................................69

Balsamic Roasted Mushrooms 69
Spinach & Bell Pepper Salad 69
Mascarpone Sweet Potato Mash 70
Rosemary Garlic Infused Olive Oil 70
Cheesy Peach And Walnut Salad 70
Cheesy Roasted Broccolini 71
Warm Kale Salad With Red Bell Pepper 71
Mediterranean Tomato Hummus Soup 72

Classic Aioli 72
Effortless Bell Pepper Salad 72
Pecorino Zucchini Strips 73
Balsamic Potato Salad With Capers 73
Spinach & Cherry Tomato Salad 73
Cucumber Salad With Goat Cheese 74
Garlic Wilted Greens 74

Fruits , Desserts And Snacks Recipes 75

Mint-watermelon Gelato 76
Grilled Pesto Halloumi Cheese 76
Cantaloupe & Watermelon Balls 77
Coconut Blueberries With Brown Rice 77
Dark Chocolate Barks 78
Hummus & Tomato Stuffed Cucumbers 78
Chive Ricotta Spread 78
Fruit Skewers With Vanilla Labneh 79
Strawberries With Balsamic Vinegar 79
Wrapped Pears In Prosciutto 79
Fruit And Nut Chocolate Bark 80
5-minute Avocado Spread 80
Kid´s Marzipan Balls 81
Simple Apple Compote 81
Charred Asparagus 81
Easy Mixed Berry Crisp 82
Speedy Granita 82
Berry Sorbet 83
Fancy Baileys Ice Coffee 83
Apple And Berries Ambrosia 83
Pesto & Egg Avocado Boats 84
Charred Maple Pineapple 84
Honey & Spice Roasted Almonds 84
Balsamic Strawberry Caprese Skewers 85
Dates Stuffed With Mascarpone & Almonds 85
Strawberry Parfait 85
Minty Yogurt & Banana Cups 86

Crispy Sesame Cookies 86
Chocolate, Almond, And Cherry Clusters 87
Shallot & Kale Spread 87
Pesto Arugula Dip 87
Choco-tahini Glazed Apple Chips 88
Pomegranate Blueberry Granita 88
Prawn & Cucumber Bites 89
Crispy Kale Chips 89
Cardamom Apple Slices 89
Crispy Potato Chips 90
Pecan & Raspberry & Frozen Yogurt Cups 90
Iberian Spread For Sandwiches 90
Mini Cucumber & Cream Cheese Sandwiches . 91
Skillet Pesto Pizza 91
Sicilian Almond Granita 92
Glazed Pears With Hazelnuts 92
Fig & Mascarpone Toasts With Pistachios 93
Italian Submarine-style Sandwiches 93
Garlic-yogurt Dip With Walnuts 93
Crunchy Almond Cookies 94
Grilled Stone Fruit With Honey 94
Goat Cheese Dip With Scallions & Lemon 95
Savory Cauliflower Steaks 95
Thyme Lentil Spread 95
Baked Beet Fries With Feta Cheese 96
Salt & Pepper Toasted Walnuts 96

30 Day Meal Plan 97

Appendix : Recipes Index 99

Few years ago, I was texting with my best friend about life and discuss how "healthy" she was. She always stay up late and never go to the gym doing exercise. One day she was diagnosed with stomach cancer. Luckily, it was not as serious as we thought. She went through surgery and get better.

I never forget the moment she was sent into the surgery room, and said something unforgettable to me. She said that we all come to the world and will leave the world, we need to do something important to us so that we will not be regret.

In later time, I accidentally found a diet called the Mediterranean Diet which is healthy especially for my best friend. I dive into it and search as much information as I could. I looked up cancer patients on a Mediterranean diet, some of them had an increased chance of surviving especially when they eat this way before or during diagnosis.

It's interesting how I saw her as normal person before, then suddenly not healthy at all and living with cancer. But now I see her as healthy again but more health-conscious now than ever before - because she fought for her life and won!

This diet cookbook is the important thing I will not be regret. If it can help you in some way, it would be the most successful thing I have ever done. In this diet cookbook, it will have an introduction with information about the diet, as well as some of its most healthy recipes. It will cover things like what is the Mediterranean Diet, how to start it, what recipes in it that are considered nutritious.

I hope that these all information can help you to improve your overall health.

Get to Know Crock Pot

The Mediterranean Diet was the Best Overall Diet in 2022, 2021, 2020, 2019, and 2018, according to U.S. News & World Report. Also, the Mediterranean diet was named the best plant-based diet, best heart-healthy diet, best diabetes diet, best diet for healthy eating, and the easiest diet to follow in 2022.

In 1993 Oldways created the Mediterranean Diet Pyramid - in partnership with the Harvard School of Public

Health and the WHO - as a healthier alternative to the USDA's original food pyramid. With fresh studies highlighting its advantages every month and a growing acceptance of Mediterranean products and flavors among home cooks and chefs alike, the Mediterranean Diet is more well-known than ever before.

The health advantages of the Mediterranean diet have been studied for years. Diets low in processed foods and high in fruits, vegetables, seafood, and healthy fats are good for us in general and for our hearts in particular.

It has been demonstrated that following a diet similar to that practiced in regions like areas of the Middle East, Greece, Italy, and Crete lowers the chance of developing heart disease. Additionally, it lowers the risk of developing chronic inflammatory disorders like Parkinson's, Alzheimer's, and cancer. The diet is another suggestion for managing diabetes from the American Diabetes Association (ADA)Reliable Source.

The Mediterranean diet draws upon the culinary practices of southern Europe, North Africa, and the Mediterranean Middle East. This eating plan consists primarily of foods available geographically in those regions prior to globalization. The initial dietary regimen featured fresh, locally sourced items that were in season.

The historic eating habits of residents of Mediterranean nations like Greece, Spain, and Italy are the foundation of the Mediterranean diet. Generally, the diet includes lots of fruits, veggies, whole grains, nuts, seeds, fish, and heart-healthy fats, such as olive oil. Along with moderate amounts of chicken, eggs, and dairy items, red wine is also acceptable. While on a diet you should stay away from refined grains, highly processed foods, and foods or drinks with a lot of added sugar.

The Mediterranean Diet contains many different nutrients working together to help your body. There's no single food or ingredient responsible for the Mediterranean Diet's benefits. Instead, the diet is good for you because it provides combination of nutrients.

An analysis on the Mediterranean diet shows that the greater an individual's adherence to this dietary pattern, the more significant the benefit to their overall health. Those who closely followed a Mediterranean diet showed a considerable decline in: overall mortality by 9%, reduction of mortality from cardiovascular diseases by 9%, the incidence of or mortality from cancer by 6%, and the incidence of Parkinson's and Alzheimer's diseases by 13%.

Additionally, studies show that those who eat a Mediterranean-style diet see improvements in their blood pressure, blood sugar, cholesterol, cognitive performance, and even sleep.

With so many tasty and flavorful food options available, the Mediterranean diet is the opposite of restrictive, boring, and flavorless, making it easier to incorporate as part of a healthy lifestyle.

BASIC KITCHEN CONVERSIONS & EQUIVALENTS

DRY MEASUREMENTS CONVERSION CHART

3 TEASPOONS = 1 TABLESPOON = 1/16 CUP

6 TEASPOONS = 2 TABLESPOONS = 1/8 CUP

12 TEASPOONS = 4 TABLESPOONS = 1/4 CUP

24 TEASPOONS = 8 TABLESPOONS = 1/2 CUP

36 TEASPOONS = 12 TABLESPOONS = 3/4 CUP

48 TEASPOONS = 16 TABLESPOONS = 1 CUP

METRIC TO US COOKING CONVERSIONS

OVEN TEMPERATURES

120 °C = 250 °F

160 °C = 320 °F

180° C = 350 °F

205 °C = 400 °F

220 °C = 425 °F

LIQUID MEASUREMENTS CONVERSION CHART

8 FLUID OUNCES = 1 CUP = 1/2 PINT = 1/4 QUART

16 FLUID OUNCES = 2 CUPS = 1 PINT = 1/2 QUART

32 FLUID OUNCES = 4 CUPS = 2 PINTS = 1 QUART = 1/4 GALLON

128 FLUID OUNCES = 16 CUPS = 8 PINTS = 4 QUARTS = 1 GALLON

BAKING IN GRAMS

1 CUP FLOUR = 140 GRAMS

1 CUP SUGAR = 150 GRAMS

1 CUP POWDERED SUGAR = 160 GRAMS

1 CUP HEAVY CREAM = 235 GRAMS

VOLUME

1 MILLILITER = 1/5 TEASPOON

5 ML = 1 TEASPOON

15 ML = 1 TABLESPOON

240 ML = 1 CUP OR 8 FLUID OUNCES

1 LITER = 34 FL. OUNCES

WEIGHT

1 GRAM = .035 OUNCES

100 GRAMS = 3.5 OUNCES

500 GRAMS = 1.1 POUNDS

1 KILOGRAM = 35 OUNCES

US TO METRIC COOKING CONVERSIONS

1/5 TSP = 1 ML

1 TSP = 5 ML

1 TBSP = 15 ML

1 FL OUNCE = 30 ML

1 CUP = 237 ML

1 PINT (2 CUPS) = 473 ML

1 QUART (4 CUPS) = .95 LITER

1 GALLON (16 CUPS) = 3.8 LITERS

1 OZ = 28 GRAMS

1 POUND = 454 GRAMS

BUTTER

1 CUP BUTTER = 2 STICKS = 8 OUNCES = 230 GRAMS = 8 TABLESPOONS

WHAT DOES 1 CUP EQUAL

1 CUP = 8 FLUID OUNCES

1 CUP = 16 TABLESPOONS

1 CUP = 48 TEASPOONS

1 CUP = 1/2 PINT

1 CUP = 1/4 QUART

1 CUP = 1/16 GALLON

1 CUP = 240 ML

BAKING PAN CONVERSIONS

1 CUP ALL-PURPOSE FLOUR = 4.5 OZ

1 CUP ROLLED OATS = 3 OZ 1 LARGE EGG = 1.7 OZ

1 CUP BUTTER = 8 OZ 1 CUP MILK = 8 OZ

1 CUP HEAVY CREAM = 8.4 OZ

1 CUP GRANULATED SUGAR = 7.1 OZ

1 CUP PACKED BROWN SUGAR = 7.75 OZ

1 CUP VEGETABLE OIL = 7.7 OZ

1 CUP UNSIFTED POWDERED SUGAR = 4.4 OZ

BAKING PAN CONVERSIONS

9-INCH ROUND CAKE PAN = 12 CUPS

10-INCH TUBE PAN =16 CUPS

11-INCH BUNDT PAN = 12 CUPS

9-INCH SPRINGFORM PAN = 10 CUPS

9 X 5 INCH LOAF PAN = 8 CUPS

9-INCH SQUARE PAN = 8 CUPS

Breakfast Recipes

Breakfast Recipes

Eggs Florentine With Pancetta

Servings:2 | Cooking Time:20 Minutes

Ingredients:

- 1 English muffin, toasted and halved
- ¼ cup chopped pancetta
- 2 tsp hollandaise sauce
- 1 cup spinach
- Salt and black pepper to taste
- 2 large eggs

Directions:

1. Place pancetta in a pan over medium heat and cook for 5 minutes until crispy; reserve. Add the baby spinach and cook for 2-3 minutes in the same pan until the spinach wilts. Fill a pot with 3 inches of water over medium heat and bring to a boil. Add 1 tbsp of vinegar and reduce the heat.
2. Crack the eggs one at a time into a small dish and gently pour into the simmering water. Poach the eggs for 2-3 minutes until the whites are set, but the yolks are still soft; remove with a slotted spoon. Divide the spinach between muffin halves and top with pancetta and poached eggs. Spoon the hollandaise sauce on top and serve.

Nutrition Info:

- Per Serving: Calories: 173;Fat: 7g;Protein: 11g;Carbs: 17g.

Easy Buckwheat Porridge

Servings:4 | Cooking Time: 40 Minutes

Ingredients:

- 3 cups water
- 2 cups raw buckwheat groats
- Pinch sea salt
- 1 cup unsweetened almond milk

Directions:

1. In a medium saucepan, add the water, buckwheat groats, and sea salt and bring to a boil over medium-high heat.
2. Once it starts to boil, reduce the heat to low. Cook for about 20 minutes, stirring occasionally, or until most of the water is absorbed.
3. Fold in the almond milk and whisk well. Continue cooking for about 15 minutes, or until the buckwheat groats are very softened.
4. Ladle the porridge into bowls and serve warm.

Nutrition Info:

- Per Serving: Calories: 121;Fat: 1.0g;Protein: 6.3g;Carbs: 21.5g.

Pecan & Peach Parfait

Servings:2 | Cooking Time:15 Minutes

Ingredients:

- 1 ½ cups Greek yogurt
- ½ cup pecans
- ½ cup whole-grain rolled oats
- 1 tsp honey
- 1 peeled and chopped peach
- Mint leaves for garnish

Directions:

1. Preheat oven to 310 °F. Pour the oats and pecans into a baking sheet and spread evenly. Toast for 11-13 minutes; set aside. Microwave honey for 30 seconds. Stir in the peach.
2. Divide some peach mixture between 2 glasses, spread some yogurt on top, and sprinkle with the oat mixture. Repeat the layering process to exhaust the ingredients, finishing with the peach mixture. Serve with mint leaves.

Nutrition Info:

- Per Serving: Calories: 403;Fat: 19g;Protein: 22g;Carbs: 40g.

Cinnamon Oatmeal With Dried Cranberries

Servings:2 | Cooking Time: 8 Minutes

Ingredients:

- 1 cup almond milk
- 1 cup water
- Pinch sea salt
- 1 cup old-fashioned oats
- ½ cup dried cranberries
- 1 teaspoon ground cinnamon

Directions:

1. In a medium saucepan over high heat, bring the almond milk, water, and salt to a boil.
2. Stir in the oats, cranberries, and cinnamon. Reduce the heat to medium and cook for 5 minutes, stirring occasionally.
3. Remove the oatmeal from the heat. Cover and let it stand for 3 minutes. Stir before serving.

Nutrition Info:

- Per Serving: Calories: 107;Fat: 2.1g;Protein: 3.2g;Carbs: 18.2g.

Creamy Vanilla Oatmeal

Servings:4 | Cooking Time: 40 Minutes

Ingredients:

- 4 cups water
- Pinch sea salt
- 1 cup steel-cut oats
- ¾ cup unsweetened almond milk
- 2 teaspoons pure vanilla extract

Directions:

1. Add the water and salt to a large saucepan over high heat and bring to a boil.
2. Once boiling, reduce the heat to low and add the oats. Mix well and cook for 30 minutes, stirring occasionally.
3. Fold in the almond milk and vanilla and whisk to combine. Continue cooking for about 10 minutes, or until the oats are thick and creamy.
4. Ladle the oatmeal into bowls and serve warm.

Nutrition Info:

- Per Serving: Calories: 117;Fat: 2.2g;Protein: 4.3g;Carbs: 20.0g.

Cheese & Mushroom Muffins

Servings:6 | Cooking Time:40 Minutes

Ingredients:

- 6 eggs
- Salt and black pepper to taste
- 1 cup Gruyere cheese, grated
- 1 yellow onion, chopped
- 1 cup mushrooms, sliced
- ½ cup green olives, chopped

Directions:

1. Beat the eggs, salt, pepper, Gruyere cheese, onion, mushrooms, and green olives in a bowl. Pour into a silicone muffin tray and bake for 30 minutes at 360 F. Serve warm.

Nutrition Info:

- Per Serving: Calories: 120;Fat: 6g;Protein: 8g;Carbs: 10g.

Avocado Toast With Goat Cheese

Servings:2 | Cooking Time: 2 To 3 Minutes

Ingredients:

- 2 slices whole-wheat thin-sliced bread
- ½ avocado
- 2 tablespoons crumbled goat cheese
- Salt, to taste

Directions:

1. Toast the bread slices in a toaster for 2 to 3 minutes on each side until browned.
2. Scoop out the flesh from the avocado into a medium bowl and mash it with a fork to desired consistency. Spread the mash onto each piece of toast.
3. Scatter the crumbled goat cheese on top and season as needed with salt.
4. Serve immediately.

Nutrition Info:

- Per Serving: Calories: 136;Fat: 5.9g;Protein: 5.0g;Carbs: 17.5g.

Cream Peach Smoothie

Servings:1 | Cooking Time:5 Minutes

Ingredients:

- 1 large peach, sliced
- 6 oz peach Greek yogurt
- 2 tbsp almond milk
- 2 ice cubes

Directions:

1. Blend the peach, yogurt, almond milk, and ice cubes in your food processor until thick and creamy. Serve and enjoy!

Nutrition Info:

- Per Serving: Calories: 228;Fat: 3g;Protein: 11g;Carbs: 41.6g.

Raspberry-yogurt Smoothie

Servings:2 | Cooking Time:10 Minutes

Ingredients:

- 2 cups raspberries
- 1 tsp honey
- 1 cup natural yogurt
- ½ cup milk
- 8 ice cubes

Directions:

1. In a food processor, combine yogurt, raspberries, honey, and milk. Blitz until smooth. Add in ice cubes and pulse until uniform. Serve right away.

Nutrition Info:

- Per Serving: Calories: 187;Fat: 7g;Protein: 8g;Carbs: 26g.

Mango-yogurt Smoothie

Servings:2 | Cooking Time:5 Minutes

Ingredients:

- 6 oz Greek yogurt
- 2 mangoes, chopped
- 2 tbsp milk
- 7-8 ice cubes

Directions:

1. In a food processor, place the mango, milk, yogurt, and ice cubes. Pulse until creamy and smooth. Serve right away.

Nutrition Info:

- Per Serving: Calories: 261;Fat: 2g;Protein: 12g;Carbs: 54g.

Chili & Cheese Frittata

Servings:6 | Cooking Time:35 Minutes

Ingredients:

- 2 tbsp olive oil
- 12 fresh eggs
- ¼ cup half-and-half
- Salt and black pepper to taste
- ½ chili pepper, minced
- 2 ½ cups shredded mozzarella

Directions:

1. Preheat oven to 350 °F. Whisk the eggs in a bowl. Add the half-and-half, salt, and black and stir to combine. Warm the olive oil in a skillet over medium heat. Sauté the chili pepper for 2-3 minutes. Sprinkle evenly with mozzarella cheese. Pour eggs over cheese in the skillet. Place the skillet in the oven and bake for 20–25 minutes until just firm. Let cool the frittata for a few minutes and cut into wedges. Serve hot.

Nutrition Info:

- Per Serving: Calories: 381;Fat: 31g;Protein: 25g;Carbs: 2g.

Maple Peach Smoothie

Servings:2 | Cooking Time:5 Minutes

Ingredients:

- 2 cups almond milk
- 2 cups peaches, chopped
- 1 cup crushed ice
- ½ tsp ground ginger
- 1 tbsp maple syrup

Directions:

1. In a food processor, mix milk, peaches, ice, maple syrup, and ginger until smooth. Serve.

Nutrition Info:

- Per Serving: Calories: 639;Fat: 58g;Protein: 7g;Carbs: 34.2g.

One-pan Tomato-basil Eggs

Servings:2 | Cooking Time:25 Minutes

Ingredients:

- 2 tsp olive oil
- 2 eggs, whisked
- 2 tomatoes, cubed
- 1 tbsp basil, chopped
- 1 green onion, chopped
- Salt and black pepper to taste

Directions:

1. Warm the oil in a skillet over medium heat and sauté tomatoes, green onion, salt, and pepper for 5 minutes. Stir in eggs and cook for another 10 minutes. Serve topped with basil.

Nutrition Info:

- Per Serving: Calories: 310;Fat: 15g;Protein: 12g;Carbs: 18g.

Lime Watermelon Yogurt Smoothie

Servings:6 | Cooking Time:5 Minutes

Ingredients:

- ½ cup almond milk
- 2 cups watermelon, cubed
- ½ cup Greek yogurt
- ½ tsp lime zest

Directions:

1. In a food processor, blend watermelon, almond milk, lime zest, and yogurt until smooth. Serve into glasses.

Nutrition Info:

- Per Serving: Calories: 260;Fat: 10g;Protein: 2g;Carbs: 6g.

Maple-vanilla Yogurt With Walnuts

Servings:4 | Cooking Time:10 Minutes

Ingredients:

- 2 cups Greek yogurt
- ¾ cup maple syrup
- 1 cup walnuts, chopped
- 1 tsp vanilla extract
- 2 tsp cinnamon powder

Directions:

1. Combine yogurt, walnuts, vanilla, maple syrup, and cinnamon powder in a bowl. Let sit in the fridge for 10 minutes.

Nutrition Info:

- Per Serving: Calories: 400;Fat: 25g;Protein: 11g;Carbs: 40g.

Tomato And Egg Breakfast Pizza

Servings:2 | Cooking Time: 15 Minutes

Ingredients:

- 2 slices of whole-wheat naan bread
- 2 tablespoons prepared pesto
- 1 medium tomato, sliced
- 2 large eggs

Directions:

1. Heat a large nonstick skillet over medium-high heat. Place the naan bread in the skillet and let warm for about 2 minutes on each side, or until softened.
2. Spread 1 tablespoon of the pesto on one side of each slice and top with tomato slices.
3. Remove from the skillet and place each one on its own plate.
4. Crack the eggs into the skillet, keeping them separated, and cook until the whites are no longer translucent and the yolk is cooked to desired doneness.
5. Using a spatula, spoon one egg onto each bread slice. Serve warm.

Nutrition Info:

- Per Serving: Calories: 429;Fat: 16.8g;Protein: 18.1g;Carbs: 12.0g.

Oven-baked Mozzarella Cheese Cups

Servings:2 | Cooking Time:20 Minutes

Ingredients:

- 2 eggs, whisked
- 1 tbsp chives, chopped
- 1 tbsp dill, chopped
- Salt and black pepper to taste
- 3 tbsp mozzarella, grated
- 1 tomato, chopped

Directions:

1. Preheat the oven to 400 °F. Grease 2 ramekins with cooking spray. Whisk eggs, tomato, mozzarella cheese, salt, pepper, dill, and chives in a bowl. Share into each ramekin and bake for 10 minutes. Serve warm.

Nutrition Info:

- Per Serving: Calories: 110;Fat: 8g;Protein: 8g;Carbs: 3g.

Hot Zucchini & Egg Nests

Servings:4 | Cooking Time:25 Minutes

Ingredients:

- 2 tbsp olive oil
- 4 eggs
- 1 lb zucchinis, shredded
- Salt and black pepper to taste
- ½ red chili pepper, minced
- 2 tbsp parsley, chopped

Directions:

1. Preheat the oven to 360 °F. Combine zucchini, salt, pepper, and olive oil in a bowl. Form nest shapes with a spoon onto a greased baking sheet. Crack an egg into each nest and season with salt, pepper, and chili pepper. Bake for 11 minutes. Serve topped with parsley.

Nutrition Info:

- Per Serving: Calories: 141;Fat: 11.6g;Protein: 7g;Carbs: 4.2g.

Easy Zucchini & Egg Stuffed Tomatoes

Servings:4 | Cooking Time:40 Minutes

Ingredients:

- 1 tbsp olive oil
- 1 small zucchini, grated
- 8 tomatoes, insides scooped
- 8 eggs
- Salt and black pepper to taste

Directions:

1. Preheat the oven to 360 °F. Place tomatoes on a greased baking dish. Mix the zucchini with olive oil, salt, and pepper. Divide the mixture between the tomatoes and crack an egg on each one. Bake for 20-25 minutes. Serve warm.

Nutrition Info:

- Per Serving: Calories: 280;Fat: 22g;Protein: 14g;Carbs: 12g.

Basic Tortilla De Patatas

Servings:4 | Cooking Time:35 Minutes

Ingredients:

- 1 ½ lb gold potatoes, peeled and sliced
- ½ cup olive oil
- 1 sweet onion, thinly sliced
- 8 eggs
- ½ dried oregano
- Salt to taste

Directions:

1. Heat the olive oil in a skillet over medium heat. Fry the potatoes for 8-10 minutes, stirring often. Add in onion, oregano, and salt and cook for 5-6 minutes until the potatoes are tender and slightly golden; set aside.
2. In a bowl, beat the eggs with a pinch of salt. Add in the potato mixture and mix well. Pour into the skillet and cook for about 10-12 minutes. Flip the tortilla using a plate, and cook for 2 more minutes until nice and crispy. Slice and serve.

Nutrition Info:

- Per Serving: Calories: 440;Fat: 34g;Protein: 14g;Carbs: 22g.

Apple & Date Smoothie

Servings:1 | Cooking Time:5 Minutes

Ingredients:

- 1 apple, peeled and chopped
- ½ cup milk
- 4 dates
- 1 tsp ground cinnamon

Directions:

1. In a blender, place the milk, ½ cup of water, dates, cinnamon, and apple. Blitz until smooth. Let chill in the fridge for 30 minutes. Serve in a tall glass.

Nutrition Info:

- Per Serving: Calories: 486;Fat: 29g;Protein: 4.2g;Carbs: 63g.

Honey & Feta Frozen Yogurt

Servings:4 | Cooking Time:5 Minutes + Freezing Time

Ingredients:

- 1 tbsp honey
- 1 cup Greek yogurt
- ½ cup feta cheese, crumbled
- 2 tbsp mint leaves, chopped

Directions:

1. In a food processor, blend yogurt, honey, and feta cheese until smooth. Transfer to a wide dish, cover with plastic wrap, and put in the freezer for 2 hours or until solid. When frozen, spoon into cups, sprinkle with mint, and serve.

Nutrition Info:

- Per Serving: Calories: 170;Fat: 12g;Protein: 7g;Carbs: 13g.

Simple Mushroom Omelet

Servings:2 | Cooking Time:15 Minutes

Ingredients:

- 2 tsp olive oil, divided
- 4 eggs, beaten
- 1 cup mushrooms, sliced
- 1 garlic clove, minced
- Salt and black pepper to taste
- ¼ cup sliced onions

Directions:

1. Warm the olive oil in a frying pan over medium heat. Place in garlic, mushrooms, and onions. Cook for 6 minutes, stirring often. Season with salt and pepper. Increase the heat and cook for 3 minutes. Remove to a plate.
2. In the same pan, add in the eggs and ensure they are evenly spread. Top with the veggies. Slice into wedges and serve.

Nutrition Info:

- Per Serving: Calories: 203;Fat: 13g;Protein: 13g;Carbs: 7g.

Strawberry Basil Mascarpone Toast

Servings:2 | Cooking Time:15 Minutes

Ingredients:

- 4 fresh basil leaves, sliced into thin shreds
- 4 whole-grain bread slices, toasted
- ½ cup mascarpone cheese
- 1 tbsp honey
- 1 cup strawberries, sliced

Directions:

1. In a small bowl, combine the mascarpone and honey. Spread the mixture evenly over each slice of bread. Top with sliced strawberries and basil.

Nutrition Info:

- Per Serving: Calories: 275;Fat: 8g;Protein: 16g;Carbs: 41g.

5-ingredient Quinoa Breakfast Bowls

Servings:1 | Cooking Time: 17 Minutes

Ingredients:

- ¼ cup quinoa, rinsed
- ¾ cup water, plus additional as needed
- 1 carrot, grated
- ½ small broccoli head, finely chopped
- ¼ teaspoon salt
- 1 tablespoon chopped fresh dill

Directions:

1. Add the quinoa and water to a small pot over high heat and bring to a boil.
2. Once boiling, reduce the heat to low. Cover and cook for 5 minutes, stirring occasionally.
3. Stir in the carrot, broccoli, and salt and continue cooking for 1o to 12 minutes, or until the quinoa is cooked though and the vegetables are fork-tender. If the mixture gets too thick, you can add additional water as needed.
4. Add the dill and serve warm.

Nutrition Info:

- Per Serving: Calories: 219;Fat: 2.9g;Protein: 10.0g;Carbs: 40.8g.

Berry & Cheese Omelet

Servings:4 | Cooking Time:10 Minutes

Ingredients:

- 2 tbsp olive oil
- 6 eggs, whisked
- 1 tsp cinnamon powder
- 1 cup ricotta cheese
- 4 oz berries

Directions:

1. Whisk eggs, cinnamon powder, ricotta cheese, and berries in a bowl. Warm the olive oil in a skillet over medium heat and pour in the egg mixture. Cook for 2 minutes, turn the egg and cook for 2 minutes more. Serve immediately.

Nutrition Info:

- Per Serving: Calories: 256;Fat: 18g;Protein: 15.6g;Carbs: 7g.

Baked Eggs In Avocado

Servings:2 | Cooking Time: 10 To 15 Minutes

Ingredients:

- 1 ripe large avocado
- 2 large eggs
- Salt and freshly ground black pepper, to taste
- 4 tablespoons jarred pesto, for serving
- 2 tablespoons chopped tomato, for serving
- 2 tablespoons crumbled feta cheese, for serving (optional)

Directions:

1. Preheat the oven to 425ºF.
2. Slice the avocado in half, remove the pit and scoop out a generous tablespoon of flesh from each half to create a hole big enough to fit an egg.
3. Transfer the avocado halves (cut-side up) to a baking sheet.
4. Crack 1 egg into each avocado half and sprinkle with salt and pepper.
5. Bake in the preheated oven for 10 to 15 minutes, or until the eggs are cooked to your preferred doneness.
6. Remove the avocado halves from the oven. Scatter each avocado half evenly with the jarred pesto, chopped tomato, and crumbled feta cheese (if desired). Serve immediately.

Nutrition Info:

- Per Serving: Calories: 301;Fat: 25.9g;Protein: 8.1g;Carbs: 9.8g.

Maple Berry & Walnut Oatmeal

Servings:2 | Cooking Time:10 Minutes

Ingredients:

- 1 cup mixed berries
- 1 ½ cups rolled oats
- 2 tbsp walnuts, chopped
- 2 tsp maple syrup

Directions:

1. Cook the oats according to the package instructions and share in 2 bowls. Microwave the maple syrup and berries for 30 seconds; stir well. Pour over each bowl. Top with walnuts.

Nutrition Info:

- Per Serving: Calories: 262;Fat: 10g;Protein: 15g;Carbs: 57g.

Berry-yogurt Smoothie

Servings:1 | Cooking Time:5 Minutes

Ingredients:

- ½ cup Greek yogurt
- ¼ cup milk
- ½ cup fresh blueberries
- 1 tsp vanilla sugar
- 2 ice cubes

Directions:

1. Pulse the Greek yogurt, milk, vanilla sugar, and berries in your blender until the berries are liquefied. Add the ice cubes and blend on high until thick and smooth. Serve.

Nutrition Info:

- Per Serving: Calories: 230;Fat: 8.8g;Protein: 16g;Carbs: 23g.

Za'atar Pizza

Servings:4 | Cooking Time: 1o To 12 Minutes

Ingredients:

- 1 sheet puff pastry
- ¼ cup extra-virgin olive oil
- ⅓ cup za'atar seasoning

Directions:

1. Preheat the oven to 350ºF. Line a baking sheet with parchment paper.
2. Place the puff pastry on the prepared baking sheet. Cut the pastry into desired slices.
3. Brush the pastry with the olive oil. Sprinkle with the za'atar seasoning.
4. Put the pastry in the oven and bake for 10 to 12 minutes, or until edges are lightly browned and puffed up.
5. Serve warm.

Nutrition Info:

- Per Serving: Calories: 374;Fat: 30.0g;Protein: 3.0g;Carbs: 20.0g.

Anchovy & Spinach Sandwiches

Servings:2 | Cooking Time:5 Minutes

Ingredients:

- 1 avocado, mashed
- 4 anchovies, drained
- 4 whole-wheat bread slices
- 1 cup baby spinach
- 1 tomato, sliced

Directions:

1. Spread the slices of bread with avocado mash and arrange the anchovies over. Top with baby spinach and tomato slices.

Nutrition Info:

- Per Serving: Calories: 300;Fat: 12g;Protein: 5g;Carbs: 10g.

Granola & Berry Parfait

Servings:2 | Cooking Time:5 Minutes

Ingredients:

- 2 cups berries
- 1 ½ cups Greek yogurt
- 1 tbsp powdered sugar
- ¼ cup granola

Directions:

1. Divide between two bowls a layer of berries, yogurt, and powdered sugar. Scatter with granola and serve.

Nutrition Info:

- Per Serving: Calories: 244;Fat: 11g;Protein: 21g;Carbs: 43g.

Beans , Grains, And Pastas Recipes

Beans , Grains, And Pastas Recipes

One-step Couscous

Servings:6 | Cooking Time:15 Minutes

Ingredients:

- 2 tbsp olive oil
- 2 cups couscous
- 1 cup water
- 1 cup vegetable broth
- Salt and black pepper to taste

Directions:

1. In a saucepan, heat the oil and add couscous. Stir until grains are just almost brown, 3-5 minutes. Stir in water, broth, and one teaspoon salt. Cover, remove the saucepan from the heat, and let sit until couscous is tender, 7 minutes. Gently fluff couscous with fork and season with pepper to taste.

Nutrition Info:

- Per Serving: Calories: 355;Fat: 6g;Protein: 8g;Carbs: 44g.

Quinoa With Baby Potatoes And Broccoli

Servings:4 | Cooking Time: 10 Minutes

Ingredients:

- 2 tablespoons olive oil
- 1 cup baby potatoes, cut in half
- 1 cup broccoli florets
- 2 cups cooked quinoa
- Zest of 1 lemon
- Sea salt and freshly ground pepper, to taste

Directions:

1. Heat the olive oil in a large skillet over medium heat until shimmering.
2. Add the potatoes and cook for about 6 to 7 minutes, or until softened and golden brown. Add the broccoli and cook for about 3 minutes, or until tender.
3. Remove from the heat and add the quinoa and lemon zest. Season with salt and pepper to taste, then serve.

Nutrition Info:

- Per Serving: Calories: 205;Fat: 8.6g;Protein: 5.1g;Carbs: 27.3g.

Spaghetti With Pine Nuts And Cheese

Servings:4 | Cooking Time: 11 Minutes

Ingredients:

- 8 ounces spaghetti
- 4 tablespoons almond butter
- 1 teaspoon freshly ground black pepper
- ½ cup pine nuts
- 1 cup fresh grated Parmesan cheese, divided

Directions:

1. Bring a large pot of salted water to a boil. Add the pasta and cook for 8 minutes.
2. In a large saucepan over medium heat, combine the butter, black pepper, and pine nuts. Cook for 2 to 3 minutes, or until the pine nuts are lightly toasted.
3. Reserve ½ cup of the pasta water. Drain the pasta and place it into the pan with the pine nuts.
4. Add ¾ cup of the Parmesan cheese and the reserved pasta water to the pasta and toss everything together to evenly coat the pasta.
5. Transfer the pasta to a serving dish and top with the remaining ¼ cup of the Parmesan cheese. Serve immediately.

Nutrition Info:

- Per Serving: Calories: 542;Fat: 32.0g;Protein: 20.0g;Carbs: 46.0g.

Swiss Chard Couscous With Feta Cheese

Servings:4 | Cooking Time:20 Minutes

Ingredients:

- 2 tbsp olive oil
- 10 oz couscous
- 2 garlic cloves, minced
- 1 cup raisins
- ½ cup feta cheese, crumbled
- 1 bunch of Swiss chard, torn

Directions:

1. In a bowl, place couscous and cover with hot water. Let sit covered for 10 minutes. Using a fork, fluff it. Warm the olive oil in a skillet over medium heat and sauté garlic for a minute. Stir in couscous, raisins, and chard. Top with feta.

Nutrition Info:

- Per Serving: Calories: 310;Fat: 8g;Protein: 7g;Carbs: 18g.

Cranberry And Almond Quinoa

Servings:2 | Cooking Time: 10 Minutes

Ingredients:

- 2 cups water
- 1 cup quinoa, rinsed
- ¼ cup salted sunflower seeds
- ½ cup slivered almonds
- 1 cup dried cranberries

Directions:

1. Combine water and quinoa in the Instant Pot.
2. Secure the lid. Select the Manual mode and set the cooking time for 10 minutes at High Pressure.
3. Once cooking is complete, do a quick pressure release. Carefully open the lid.
4. Add sunflower seeds, almonds, and dried cranberries and gently mix until well combined.
5. Serve hot.

Nutrition Info:

- Per Serving: Calories: 445;Fat: 14.8g;Protein: 15.1g;Carbs: 64.1g.

Parmesan Polenta

Servings:6 | Cooking Time:50 Minutes

Ingredients:

- 1 ½ cups coarse-ground cornmeal
- 2 tbsp olive oil
- 6 ½ cups water
- Salt and black pepper to taste
- ½ tsp baking soda
- 2 oz Pecorino cheese, grated

Directions:

1. In a large saucepan, bring water to a boil over medium heat. Stir in 1 teaspoon of salt and baking soda. Slowly pour cornmeal into water in a steady stream while stirring back and forth with a wooden spoon or rubber spatula. Bring mixture to boil, stirring constantly, about 1 minute. Reduce heat to the lowest setting and cover. After 4 minutes, whisk polenta to smooth out any lumps that may have formed, about 20 seconds. Cover and continue to cook, without stirring, until polenta grains are tender but slightly al dente, about 23 minutes longer. Off heat, stir in Pecorino and oil and season with pepper to taste. Cover and let sit for 5 minutes. Serve along with extra Pecorino cheese on the side.

Nutrition Info:

- Per Serving: Calories: 235;Fat: 18g;Protein: 11g;Carbs: 29g.

Lemon Couscous With Broccoli

Servings:4 | Cooking Time:20 Minutes

Ingredients:

- 2 tsp olive oil
- Salt and black pepper to taste
- 1 small red onion, sliced
- 1 lemon, zested
- 1 head broccoli, cut into florets
- 1 cup couscous

Directions:

1. Heat a pot filled with salted water over medium heat; bring to a boil. Add in the broccoli and cook for 4-6 minutes until tender. Remove to a boil with a slotted spoon. In another bowl, place the couscous and cover with boiling broccoli water. Cover and let sit for 3-4 minutes until the water is absorbrd. Fluff the couscous with a fork and season with lemon zest, salt. and pepper. Stir in broccoli and top with red onion to serve.

Nutrition Info:

- Per Serving: Calories: 620;Fat: 45g;Protein: 11g;Carbs: 51g.

Lemon-basil Spaghetti

Servings:6 | Cooking Time:30 Minutes

Ingredients:

- ½ cup extra-virgin olive oil
- Zest and juice from 1 lemon
- 1 garlic clove, minced
- Salt and black pepper to taste
- 2 oz ricotta cheese, chopped
- 1 lb spaghetti
- 6 tbsp shredded frcsh basil

Directions:

1. In a bowl, whisk oil, grated lemon zest, juice, garlic, salt, and pepper. Stir in ricotta cheese and mix well. Meanwhile, bring a pot filled with salted water to a boil. Cook the pasta until al dente. Reserve ½ cup of the cooking liquid, then drain pasta and return it to the pot. Add oil mixture and basil and toss to combine. Season to taste and adjust consistency with reserved cooking water as needed. Serve warm.

Nutrition Info:

- Per Serving: Calories: 395;Fat: 11g;Protein: 10g;Carbs: 37g.

Mint Brown Rice

Servings:2 | Cooking Time: 22 Minutes

Ingredients:

- 2 cloves garlic, minced
- ¼ cup chopped fresh mint, plus more for garnish
- 1 tablespoon chopped dried chives
- 1 cup short- or long-grain brown rice
- 1½ cups water or low-sodium vegetable broth
- ½ to 1 teaspoon sea salt

Directions:

1. Place the garlic, mint, chives, rice, and water in the Instant Pot. Stir to combine.
2. Secure the lid. Select the Manual mode and set the cooking time for 22 minutes at High Pressure.
3. Once cooking is complete, do a natural pressure release for 10 minutes, then release any remaining pressure. Carefully open the lid.
4. Add salt to taste. Serve garnished with more mint.

Nutrition Info:

- Per Serving: Calories: 514;Fat: 6.6g;Protein: 20.7g;Carbs: 80.4g.

Broccoli And Carrot Pasta Salad

Servings:2 | Cooking Time: 10 Minutes

Ingredients:

- 8 ounces whole-wheat pasta
- 2 cups broccoli florets
- 1 cup peeled and shredded carrots
- ¼ cup plain Greek yogurt
- Juice of 1 lemon
- 1 teaspoon red pepper flakes
- Sea salt and freshly ground pepper, to taste

Directions:

1. Bring a large pot of lightly salted water to a boil. Add the pasta to the boiling water and cook until al dente. Drain and let rest for a few minutes.
2. When cooled, combine the pasta with the veggies, yogurt, lemon juice, and red pepper flakes in a large bowl, and stir thoroughly to combine.
3. Taste and season to taste with salt and pepper. Serve immediately.

Nutrition Info:

- Per Serving: Calories: 428;Fat: 2.9g;Protein: 15.9g;Carbs: 84.6g.

Quick Pesto Pasta

Servings:4 | Cooking Time:20 Minutes

Ingredients:

- 1 lb linguine
- 2 tomatoes, chopped
- 10 oz basil pesto
- ½ cup pine nuts, toasted
- ½ cup Parmesan cheese, grated
- 1 lemon, zested

Directions:

1. Bring to a boil salted water in a pot over high heat. Add the linguine and cook according to package directions, 9-11 minutes. Drain and transfer to a serving bowl. Add the tomatoes, pesto, and lemon zest toss gently to coat the pasta. Sprinkle with Parmesan cheese and pine nuts and serve.

Nutrition Info:

- Per Serving: Calories: 617;Fat: 17g;Protein: 23g;Carbs: 94g.

Raspberry & Nut Quinoa

Servings:4 | Cooking Time:5 Minutes

Ingredients:

- 1 tbsp honey
- 2 cups almond milk
- 2 cups quinoa, cooked
- ½ tsp cinnamon powder
- 1 cup raspberries
- ¼ cup walnuts, chopped

Directions:

1. Combine quinoa, milk, cinnamon powder, honey, raspberries, and walnuts in a bowl. Serve in individual bowls.

Nutrition Info:

- Per Serving: Calories: 300;Fat: 15g;Protein: 5g;Carbs: 15g.

Poultry And Meats Recipes

Poultry And Meats Recipes

Easy Grilled Pork Chops

Servings:4 | Cooking Time: 10 Minutes

Ingredients:

- ¼ cup extra-virgin olive oil
- 2 tablespoons fresh thyme leaves
- 1 teaspoon smoked paprika
- 1 teaspoon salt
- 4 pork loin chops, ½-inch-thick

Directions:

1. In a small bowl, mix together the olive oil, thyme, paprika, and salt.
2. Put the pork chops in a plastic zip-top bag or a bowl and coat them with the spice mix. Let them marinate for 15 minutes.
3. Preheat the grill to high heat. Cook the pork chops for 4 minutes on each side until cooked through.
4. Serve warm.

Nutrition Info:

- Per Serving: Calories: 282;Fat: 23.0g;Protein: 21.0g;Carbs: 1.0g.

Peach Pork Chops

Servings:4 | Cooking Time:30 Minutes

Ingredients:

- 2 tbsp olive oil
- ½ tsp cayenne powder
- 4 pork chops, boneless
- ¼ cup peach preserves
- 1 tbsp thyme, chopped

Directions:

1. In a bowl, mix peach preserves, olive oil, and cayenne powder. Preheat your grill to medium. Rub pork chops with some peach glaze and grill for 10 minutes. Turn the chops, rub more glaze and cook for 10 minutes. Top with thyme.

Nutrition Info:

- Per Serving: Calories: 240;Fat: 12g;Protein: 24g;Carbs: 7g.

Baked Garlicky Pork Chops

Servings:4 | Cooking Time:45 Minutes

Ingredients:

- 1 tbsp olive oil
- 4 pork loin chops, boneless
- Salt and black pepper to taste
- 4 garlic cloves, minced
- 1 tbsp thyme, chopped

Directions:

1. Preheat the oven to 390° F. Place pork chops, salt, pepper, garlic, thyme, and olive oil in a roasting pan and bake for 10 minutes. Decrease the heat to 360° F and bake for 25 minutes.

Nutrition Info:

- Per Serving: Calories: 170;Fat: 6g;Protein: 26g;Carbs: 2g.

Tomato Walnut Chicken

Servings:4 | Cooking Time:35 Minutes

Ingredients:

- 2 tbsp olive oil
- 1 lb chicken breast halves
- Salt and black pepper to taste
- 2 tbsp walnuts, chopped
- 1 tbsp chives, chopped
- ½ cup tomato sauce
- ½ cup chicken stock

Directions:

1. Warm the olive oil in a skillet over medium heat and cook chicken for 8 minutes, flipping once. Season with salt and pepper. Stir in walnuts, tomato sauce, and stock and bring to a boil. Cook for 16 minutes. Serve sprinkled with chives.

Nutrition Info:

- Per Serving: Calories: 300;Fat: 13g;Protein: 36g;Carbs: 26g.

Chicken Caprese

Servings:4 | Cooking Time:50 Minutes

Ingredients:

- 1 tsp garlic powder
- ½ cup basil pesto
- 4 chicken breast halves
- 3 tomatoes, sliced
- 1 cup mozzarella, shredded
- Salt and black pepper to taste

Directions:

1. Preheat the oven to 390° F. Line a baking dish with parchment paper and grease with cooking spray. Combine chicken, garlic powder, salt, pepper, and pesto in a bowl and arrange them on the sheet. Top with tomatoes and mozzarella and bake for 40 minutes. Serve hot.

Nutrition Info:

- Per Serving: Calories: 350;Fat: 21g;Protein: 33g;Carbs: 5g.

Pork Millet With Chestnuts

Servings:6 | Cooking Time:30 Minutes

Ingredients:

- 2 cups pork roast, cooked and shredded
- ½ cup sour cream
- 1 cup millet
- 3 oz water chestnuts, sliced
- Salt and white pepper to taste

Directions:

1. Place millet and salted water in a pot over medium heat and cook for 20 minutes. Drain and remove to a bowl to cool. When ready, add in pork, chestnuts, cream, salt, and pepper and mix to combine. Serve.

Nutrition Info:

- Per Serving: Calories: 300;Fat: 18g;Protein: 24g;Carbs: 17g.

Crispy Pesto Chicken

Servings:2 | Cooking Time: 50 Minutes

Ingredients:

- 12 ounces small red potatoes, scrubbed and diced into 1-inch pieces
- 1 tablespoon olive oil
- ½ teaspoon garlic powder
- ¼ teaspoon salt
- 1 boneless, skinless chicken breast
- 3 tablespoons prepared pesto

Directions:

1. Preheat the oven to 425ºF. Line a baking sheet with parchment paper.
2. Combine the potatoes, olive oil, garlic powder, and salt in a medium bowl. Toss well to coat.
3. Arrange the potatoes on the parchment paper and roast for 10 minutes. Flip the potatoes and roast for an additional 10 minutes.
4. Meanwhile, put the chicken in the same bowl and toss with the pesto, coating the chicken evenly.
5. Check the potatoes to make sure they are golden brown on the top and bottom. Toss them again and add the chicken breast to the pan.
6. Turn the heat down to 350ºF and roast the chicken and potatoes for 30 minutes. Check to make sure the chicken reaches an internal temperature of 165ºF and the potatoes are fork-tender.
7. Let cool for 5 minutes before serving.

Nutrition Info:

- Per Serving: Calories: 378;Fat: 16.0g;Protein: 29.8g;Carbs: 30.1g.

Grilled Beef With Mint-jalapeño Vinaigrette

Servings:4 | Cooking Time:25 Minutes

Ingredients:

- 2 tbsp olive oil
- 1 lb beef steaks
- 3 jalapeños, chopped
- 2 tbsp balsamic vinegar
- 1 cup mint leaves, chopped
- Salt and black pepper to taste
- 1 tbsp sweet paprika

Directions:

1. Warm half of oil in a skillet over medium heat and sauté jalapeños, balsamic vinegar, mint, salt, pepper, and paprika for 5 minutes. Preheat the grill to high. Rub beef steaks with the remaining oil, salt, and pepper and grill for 6 minutes on both sides. Top with mint vinaigrette and serve.

Nutrition Info:

- Per Serving: Calories: 320;Fat: 13g;Protein: 18g;Carbs: 19g.

Pork Tenderloin With Caraway Seeds

Servings:4 | Cooking Time:30 Minutes

Ingredients:

- 2 tbsp olive oil
- 1 lb pork tenderloin, sliced
- Salt and black pepper to taste
- 3 tbsp ground caraway seeds
- 1/3 cup half-and-half
- ½ cup dill, chopped

Directions:

1. Warm the olive oil in a skillet over medium heat and sear pork for 8 minutes on all sides. Stir in salt, pepper, ground caraway seeds, half-and-half, and dill and bring to a boil. Cook for another 12 minutes. Serve warm.

Nutrition Info:

- Per Serving: Calories: 330;Fat: 15g;Protein: 18g;Carbs: 15g.

Rosemary Pork Loin With Green Onions

Servings:4 | Cooking Time:50 Minutes

Ingredients:

- 2 lb pork loin roast, boneless and cubed
- 2 tbsp olive oil
- 2 garlic cloves, minced
- Salt and black pepper to taste
- 1 cup tomato sauce
- 1 tsp rosemary, chopped
- 4 green onions, chopped

Directions:

1. Preheat the oven to 360° F. Heat olive oil in a skillet over medium heat and cook pork, garlic, and green onions for 6-7 minutes, stirring often. Add in tomato sauce, rosemary, and 1 cup of water. Season with salt and pepper. Transfer to a baking dish and bake for 40 minutes. Serve warm.

Nutrition Info:

- Per Serving: Calories: 280;Fat: 16g;Protein: 19g;Carbs: 18g.

Original Meatballs

Servings:4 | Cooking Time:25 Minutes

Ingredients:

- 2 tbsp olive oil
- 1 lb ground beef meat
- 1 onion, chopped
- 3 tbsp cilantro, chopped
- 1 garlic clove, minced
- Salt and black pepper to taste

Directions:

1. Combine beef, onion, cilantro, garlic, salt, and pepper in a bowl and form meatballs out of the mixture. Sprinkle with oil. Preheat the grill over medium heat and grill them for 14 minutes on all sides. Serve with salad.

Nutrition Info:

- Per Serving: Calories: 240;Fat: 15g;Protein: 13g;Carbs: 17g.

Greek-style Lamb Burgers

Servings:4 | Cooking Time: 10 Minutes

Ingredients:

- 1 pound ground lamb
- ½ teaspoon salt
- ½ teaspoon freshly ground black pepper
- 4 tablespoons crumbled feta cheese
- Buns, toppings, and tzatziki, for serving (optional)

Directions:

1. Preheat the grill to high heat.
2. In a large bowl, using your hands, combine the lamb with the salt and pepper.
3. Divide the meat into 4 portions. Divide each portion in half to make a top and a bottom. Flatten each half into a 3-inch circle. Make a dent in the center of one of the halves and place 1 tablespoon of the feta cheese in the center. Place the second half of the patty on top of the feta cheese and press down to close the 2 halves together, making it resemble a round burger.
4. Grill each side for 3 minutes, for medium-well. Serve on a bun with your favorite toppings and tzatziki sauce, if desired.

Nutrition Info:

- Per Serving: Calories: 345;Fat: 29.0g;Protein: 20.0g;Carbs: 1.0g.

Creamy Beef Stew

Servings:4 | Cooking Time:35 Minutes

Ingredients:

- 2 tbsp olive oil
- 2 pears, peeled and cubed
- 1 lb beef stew meat, cubed
- 2 tbsp dill, chopped
- 2 oz heavy cream
- Salt and black pepper to taste

Directions:

1. Warm the olive oil in a skillet over medium heat and sear beef for 5 minutes. Stir in pears, dill, heavy cream, salt, and pepper and bring to a boil. Simmer for 20 minutes.

Nutrition Info:

- Per Serving: Calories: 340;Fat: 18g;Protein: 16g;Carbs: 23g.

Fish And Seafood Recipes

Fish And Seafood Recipes

Parsley Tomato Tilapia

Servings:4 | Cooking Time:20 Minutes

Ingredients:

- 2 tbsp olive oil
- 4 tilapia fillets, boneless
- ½ cup tomato sauce
- 2 tbsp parsley, chopped
- Salt and black pepper to taste

Directions:

1. Warm olive oil in a skillet over medium heat. Sprinkle tilapia with salt and pepper and cook until golden brown, flipping once, about 6 minutes. Pour in the tomato sauce and parsley and cook for an additional 4 minutes. Serve immediately.

Nutrition Info:

- Per Serving: Calories: 308;Fat: 17g;Protein: 16g;Carbs: 3g.

Dilly Haddock In Tomato Sauce

Servings:4 | Cooking Time:20 Minutes

Ingredients:

- 4 haddock fillets, boneless
- 1 cup vegetable stock
- 2 garlic cloves, minced
- 2 cups cherry tomatoes, halved
- Salt and black pepper to taste
- 2 tbsp dill, chopped

Directions:

1. In a skillet over medium heat, cook cherry tomatoes, garlic, salt, and pepper for 5 minutes. Stir in haddock fillets and vegetable stock and bring to a simmer. Cook covered for 10-12 minutes. Serve topped with dill.

Nutrition Info:

- Per Serving: Calories: 190;Fat: 2g;Protein: 35g;Carbs: 6g.

Lemony Sea Bass

Servings:4 | Cooking Time:25 Minutes

Ingredients:

- 1 tbsp butter, melted
- 4 skinless sea bass fillets
- Salt and black pepper to taste
- ½ tsp onion powder

Directions:

1. Preheat oven to 425 °F. Rub the fish with salt, pepper, and onion powder and place on a greased baking dish. Drizzle the butter all over and bake for 20 minutes or until opaque.

Nutrition Info:

- Per Serving: Calories: 159;Fat: 6g;Protein: 23.8g;Carbs: 1.2g.

Pancetta-wrapped Scallops

Servings:6 | Cooking Time:25 Minutes

Ingredients:

- 2 tsp olive oil
- 12 thin pancetta slices
- 12 medium scallops
- 2 tsp lemon juice
- 1 tsp chili powder

Directions:

1. Wrap pancetta around scallops and secure with toothpicks. Warm the olive oil in a skillet over medium heat and cook scallops for 6 minutes on all sides. Serve sprinkled with chili powder and lemon juice.

Nutrition Info:

- Per Serving: Calories: 310;Fat: 25g;Protein: 19g;Carbs: 24g.

Anchovy Spread With Avocado

Servings:2 | Cooking Time:5 Minutes

Ingredients:

- 1 avocado, peeled and pitted
- 1 tsp lemon juice
- ¼ celery stalk, chopped
- ¼ cup chopped shallots
- 2 anchovy fillets in olive oil
- Salt and black pepper to taste

Directions:

1. Combine lemon juice, avocado, celery, shallots, and anchovy fillets (with their olive oil) in a food processor. Blitz until smooth. Season with salt and black pepper. Serve.

Nutrition Info:

- Per Serving: Calories: 271;Fat: 20g;Protein: 15g;Carbs: 12g.

Peppercorn-seared Tuna Steaks

Servings:2 | Cooking Time: 10 Minutes

Ingredients:

- 2 ahi tuna steaks
- 1 teaspoon kosher salt
- ¼ teaspoon cayenne pepper
- 2 tablespoons olive oil
- 1 teaspoon whole peppercorns

Directions:

1. On a plate, Season the tuna steaks on both sides with salt and cayenne pepper.
2. In a skillet, heat the olive oil over medium-high heat until it shimmers.
3. Add the peppercorns and cook for about 5 minutes, or until they soften and pop.
4. Carefully put the tuna steaks in the skillet and sear for 1 to 2 minutes per side, depending on the thickness of the tuna steaks, or until the fish is cooked to the desired level of doneness.
5. Cool for 5 minutes before serving.

Nutrition Info:

- Per Serving: Calories: 260;Fat: 14.3g;Protein: 33.4g;Carbs: 0.2g.

Balsamic Asparagus & Salmon Roast

Servings:4 | Cooking Time:20 Minutes

Ingredients:

- 2 tbsp olive oil
- 4 salmon fillets, skinless
- 2 tbsp balsamic vinegar
- 1 lb asparagus, trimmed
- Salt and black pepper to taste

Directions:

1. Preheat the oven to 380ºF. In a roasting pan, arrange the salmon fillets and asparagus spears. Season with salt and pepper and drizzle with olive oil and balsamic vinegar; roast for 12-15 minutes. Serve warm.

Nutrition Info:

- Per Serving: Calories: 310;Fat: 16g;Protein: 21g;Carbs: 19g.

Herby Tuna Gratin

Servings:4 | Cooking Time:20 Minutes

Ingredients:

- 10 oz canned tuna, flaked
- 4 eggs, whisked
- ½ cup mozzarella, shredded
- 1 tbsp chives, chopped
- 1 tbsp parsley, chopped
- Salt and black pepper to taste

Directions:

1. Preheat the oven to 360°F. Mix tuna, eggs, chives, parsley, salt, and pepper in a bowl. Transfer to a greased baking dish and bake for 15 minutes. Scatter cheese on top and let sit for 5 minutes. Cut before serving.

Nutrition Info:

- Per Serving: Calories: 300;Fat: 15g;Protein: 7g;Carbs: 13g.

Salmon Packets

Servings:4 | Cooking Time:25 Minutes

Ingredients:

- 2 tbsp olive oil
- ½ cup apple juice
- 4 salmon fillets
- 4 tsp lemon zest
- 4 tbsp chopped parsley
- Salt and black pepper to taste

Directions:

1. Preheat oven to 380°F. Brush salmon with olive oil and season with salt and pepper. Cut four pieces of non-stick baking paper and divide the salmon between them. Top each one with apple juice, lemon zest, and parsley.
2. Wrap the paper to make packets and arrange them on a baking sheet. Cook for 15 minutes until the salmon is cooked through. Remove the packets to a serving plate, open them, and drizzle with cooking juices to serve.

Nutrition Info:

- Per Serving: Calories: 495;Fat: 21g;Protein: 55g;Carbs: 5g.

Creamy Trout Spread

Servings:4 | Cooking Time:5 Minutes

Ingredients:

- 2 tbsp olive oil
- 1 cup Greek yogurt
- 2 oz smoked trout, flaked
- 1 tbsp lemon juice
- 2 tbsp chives, chopped
- Salt and black pepper to taste

Directions:

1. Place trout, lemon juice, yogurt, chives, salt, pepper, and olive oil in a bowl and toss to combine. Serve with crackers.

Nutrition Info:

- Per Serving: Calories: 270;Fat: 5g;Protein: 8g;Carbs: 6g.

Baked Anchovies With Chili-garlic Topping

Servings:2 | Cooking Time:10 Minutes

Ingredients:

- ½ tsp red pepper flakes
- 16 canned anchovies
- 4 garlic cloves, minced
- Salt and black pepper to taste

Directions:

1. Preheat the broiler. Arrange the anchovies on a foil-lined baking dish. In a bowl, mix anchovy olive oil, garlic, salt, red flakes, and pepper and pour over anchovies. Broil for 3-4 minutes. Divide between 4 plates and drizzle with the remaining mixture from the dish. Serve and enjoy!

Nutrition Info:

- Per Serving: Calories: 103;Fat: 3g;Protein: 11g;Carbs: 5g.

Balsamic-honey Glazed Salmon

Servings:4 | Cooking Time: 8 Minutes

Ingredients:

- ½ cup balsamic vinegar
- 1 tablespoon honey
- 4 salmon fillets
- Sea salt and freshly ground pepper, to taste
- 1 tablespoon olive oil

Directions:

1. Heat a skillet over medium-high heat. Combine the vinegar and honey in a small bowl.
2. Season the salmon fillets with the sea salt and freshly ground pepper; brush with the honey-balsamic glaze.
3. Add olive oil to the skillet, and sear the salmon fillets, cooking for 3 to 4 minutes on each side until lightly browned and medium rare in the center.
4. Let sit for 5 minutes before serving.

Nutrition Info:

- Per Serving: Calories: 454;Fat: 17.3g;Protein: 65.3g;Carbs: 9.7g.

Grilled Lemon Pesto Salmon

Servings:2 | Cooking Time: 6 To 10 Minutes

Ingredients:

- 10 ounces salmon fillet
- Salt and freshly ground black pepper, to taste
- 2 tablespoons prepared pesto sauce
- 1 large fresh lemon, sliced
- Cooking spray

Directions:

1. Preheat the grill to medium-high heat. Spray the grill grates with cooking spray.
2. Season the salmon with salt and black pepper. Spread the pesto sauce on top.
3. Make a bed of fresh lemon slices about the same size as the salmon fillet on the hot grill, and place the salm- on on top of the lemon slices. Put any additional lemon slices on top of the salmon.
4. Grill the salmon for 6 to 10 minutes, or until the fish is opaque and flakes apart easily.
5. Serve hot.

Nutrition Info:

- Per Serving: Calories: 316;Fat: 21.1g;Protein: 29.0g;Carbs: 1.0g.

Salmon In Thyme Tomato Sauce

Servings:4 | Cooking Time:25 Minutes

Ingredients:

- 2 tbsp olive oil
- 4 salmon fillets, boneless
- 1 tsp thyme, chopped
- Salt and black pepper to taste
- 1 lb cherry tomatoes, halved

Directions:

1. Warm the olive oil in a skillet over medium heat and sear salmon for 6 minutes, turning once; set aside. In the same skillet, stir in cherry tomatoes for 3-4 minutes and sprinkle with thyme, salt, and pepper. Pour the sauce over the salmon.

Nutrition Info:

- Per Serving: Calories: 300;Fat: 18g;Protein: 26g;Carbs: 27g.

Glazed Broiled Salmon

Servings:4 | Cooking Time: 5 To 10 Minutes

Ingredients:

- 4 salmon fillets
- 3 tablespoons miso paste
- 2 tablespoons raw honey
- 1 teaspoon coconut aminos
- 1 teaspoon rice vinegar

Directions:

1. Preheat the broiler to High. Line a baking dish with aluminum foil and add the salmon fillets.
2. Whisk together the miso paste, honey, coconut aminos, and vinegar in a small bowl. Pour the glaze over the fillets and spread it evenly with a brush.
3. Broil for about 5 minutes, or until the salmon is browned on top and opaque. Brush any remaining glaze over the salmon and broil for an additional 5 minutes if needed. The cooking time depends on the thickness of the salmon.
4. Let the salmon cool for 5 minutes before serving.

Nutrition Info:

- Per Serving: Calories: 263;Fat: 8.9g;Protein: 30.2g;Carbs: 12.8g.

Rosemary Wine Poached Haddock

Servings:4 | Cooking Time:40 Minutes

Ingredients:

- 4 haddock fillets
- Salt and black pepper to taste
- 2 garlic cloves, minced
- ½ cup dry white wine
- ½ cup seafood stock
- 4 rosemary sprigs for garnish

Directions:

1. Preheat oven to 380 °F. Sprinkle haddock fillets with salt and black pepper and arrange them on a baking dish. Pour in the wine, garlic, and stock. Bake covered for 20 minutes until the fish is tender; remove to a serving plate. Pour the cooking liquid into a pot over high heat. Cook for 10 minutes until reduced by half. Place on serving dishes and top with the reduced poaching liquid. Serve garnished with rosemary.

Nutrition Info:

- Per Serving: Calories: 215;Fat: 4g;Protein: 35g;Carbs: 3g.

Crunchy Pollock Fillets

Servings:4 | Cooking Time:25 Minutes

Ingredients:

- 4 pollock fillets, boneless
- 2 cups potato chips, crushed
- 2 tbsp mayonnaise

Directions:

1. Preheat the oven to 380°F. Line a baking sheet with parchment paper. Rub each fillet with mayonnaise and dip them in the potato chips. Place fillets on the sheet and bake for 12 minutes. Serve with salad.

Nutrition Info:

- Per Serving: Calories: 240;Fat: 9g;Protein: 26g;Carbs: 10g.

Crab Stuffed Celery Sticks

Servings:4 | Cooking Time:10 Minutes

Ingredients:

- 1 cup cream cheese
- 6 oz crab meat
- 1 tsp Mediterranean seasoning
- 2 tbsp apple cider vinegar
- 8 celery sticks, halved
- Salt and black pepper to taste

Directions:

1. In a mixing bowl, combine the cream cheese, crab meat, apple cider vinegar, salt, pepper, and Mediterranean seasoning. Divide the crab mixture between the celery sticks. Serve.

Nutrition Info:

- Per Serving: Calories: 30;Fat: 2g;Protein: 3g;Carbs: 1g.

Baked Salmon With Basil And Tomato

Servings:2 | Cooking Time: 20 Minutes

Ingredients:

- 2 boneless salmon fillets
- 1 tablespoon dried basil
- 1 tomato, thinly sliced
- 1 tablespoon olive oil
- 2 tablespoons grated Parmesan cheese
- Nonstick cooking spray

Directions:

1. Preheat the oven to 375°F. Line a baking sheet with a piece of aluminum foil and mist with nonstick cooking spray.
2. Arrange the salmon fillets onto the aluminum foil and scatter with basil. Place the tomato slices on top and drizzle with olive oil. Top with the grated Parmesan cheese.
3. Bake for about 20 minutes, or until the flesh is opaque and it flakes apart easily.
4. Remove from the oven and serve on a plate.

Nutrition Info:

- Per Serving: Calories: 403;Fat: 26.5g;Protein: 36.3g;Carbs: 3.8g.

Simple Fried Cod Fillets

Servings:4 | Cooking Time: 10 Minutes

Ingredients:

- ½ cup all-purpose flour
- 1 teaspoon garlic powder
- 1 teaspoon salt
- 4 cod fillets
- 1 tablespoon extra-virgin olive oil

Directions:

1. Mix together the flour, garlic powder, and salt in a shallow dish.
2. Dredge each piece of fish in the seasoned flour until they are evenly coated.
3. Heat the olive oil in a medium skillet over medium-high heat.
4. Once hot, add the cod fillets and fry for 6 to 8 minutes, flipping the fish halfway through, or until the fish is opaque and flakes easily.
5. Remove from the heat and serve on plates.

Nutrition Info:

- Per Serving: Calories: 333;Fat: 18.8g;Protein: 21.2g;Carbs: 20.0g.

Instant Pot Poached Salmon

Servings:4 | Cooking Time: 3 Minutes

Ingredients:

- 1 lemon, sliced ¼ inch thick
- 4 skinless salmon fillets, 1½ inches thick
- ½ teaspoon salt
- ¼ teaspoon pepper
- ½ cup water

Directions:

1. Layer the lemon slices in the bottom of the Instant Pot.
2. Season the salmon with salt and pepper, then arrange the salmon (skin- side down) on top of the lemon slices. Pour in the water.
3. Secure the lid. Select the Manual mode and set the cooking time for 3 minutes at High Pressure.
4. Once cooking is complete, do a quick pressure release. Carefully open the lid.
5. Serve warm.

Nutrition Info:

- Per Serving: Calories: 350;Fat: 23.0g;Protein: 35.0g;Carbs: 0g.

Traditional Tuscan Scallops

Servings:4 | Cooking Time:25 Minutes

Ingredients:

- 2 tbsp olive oil
- 1 lb sea scallops, rinsed
- 4 cups Tuscan kale
- 1 orange, juiced
- Salt and black pepper to taste
- ¼ tsp red pepper flakes

Directions:

1. Sprinkle scallops with salt and pepper.
2. Warm olive oil in a skillet over medium heat and brown scallops for 6-8 minutes on all sides. Remove to a plate and keep warm, covering with foil. In the same skillet, add the kale, red pepper flakes, orange juice, salt, and pepper and cook until the kale wilts, about 4-5 minutes. Share the kale mixture into 4 plates and top with the scallops. Serve warm.

Nutrition Info:

- Per Serving: Calories: 214;Fat: 8g;Protein: 21g;Carbs: 15.2g.

Crispy Sole Fillets

Servings:4 | Cooking Time:10 Minutes

Ingredients:

- ¼ cup olive oil
- ½ cup flour
- ½ tsp paprika
- 8 skinless sole fillets
- Salt and black pepper to taste
- 4 lemon wedges

Directions:

1. Warm the olive oil in a skillet over medium heat. Mix the flour with paprika in a shallow dish. Coat the fish with the flour, shaking off any excess. Sear the sole fillets for 2-3 minutes per side until lightly browned. Serve with lemon wedges.

Nutrition Info:

- Per Serving: Calories: 219;Fat: 15g;Protein: 8.7g;Carbs: 13g.

Lemon-garlic Sea Bass

Servings:2 | Cooking Time:25 Minutes

Ingredients:

- 2 tbsp olive oil
- 2 sea bass fillets
- 1 lemon, juiced
- 4 garlic cloves, minced
- Salt and black pepper to taste

Directions:

1. Preheat the oven to 380°F. Line a baking sheet with parchment paper. Brush sea bass fillets with lemon juice, olive oil, garlic, salt, and pepper and arrange them on the sheet. Bake for 15 minutes. Serve with salad.

Nutrition Info:

- Per Serving: Calories: 530;Fat: 30g;Protein: 54g;Carbs: 15g.

Baked Lemon Salmon

Servings:4 | Cooking Time: 20 Minutes

Ingredients:

- ¼ teaspoon dried thyme
- Zest and juice of ½ lemon
- ¼ teaspoon salt
- ½ teaspoon freshly ground black pepper
- 1 pound salmon fillet
- Nonstick cooking spray

Directions:

1. Preheat the oven to 425ºF. Coat a baking sheet with nonstick cooking spray.
2. Mix together the thyme, lemon zest and juice, salt, and pepper in a small bowl and stir to incorporate.
3. Arrange the salmon, skin-side down, on the coated baking sheet. Spoon the thyme mixture over the salmon and spread it all over.
4. Bake in the preheated oven for about 15 to 20 minutes, or until the fish flakes apart easily. Serve warm.

Nutrition Info:

- Per Serving: Calories: 162;Fat: 7.0g;Protein: 23.1g;Carbs: 1.0g.

Baked Haddock With Rosemary Gremolata

Servings:6 | Cooking Time:35 Min + Marinating Time

Ingredients:

- 1 cup milk
- Salt and black pepper to taste
- 2 tbsp rosemary, chopped
- 1 garlic clove, minced
- 1 lemon, zested
- 1 ½ lb haddock fillets

Directions:

1. In a large bowl, coat the fish with milk, salt, pepper, and 1 tablespoon of rosemary. Refrigerate for 2 hours.
2. Preheat oven to 380ºF. Carefully remove the haddock from the marinade, drain thoroughly, and place in a greased baking dish. Cover and bake 15–20 minutes until the fish is flaky. Remove fish from the oven and let it rest 5 minutes. To make the gremolata, mix the remaining rosemary, lemon zest, and garlic. Sprinkle the fish with gremolata and serve.

Nutrition Info:

- Per Serving: Calories: 112;Fat: 2g;Protein: 20g;Carbs: 3g.

Oil–poached Cod

Servings:4 | Cooking Time:20 Minutes

Ingredients:

- 4 cod fillets, skins removed
- 3 cups olive oil
- Salt and black pepper to taste
- 1 lemon, zested and juiced
- 3 fresh thyme sprigs

Directions:

1. Heat the olive oil with thyme sprigs in a pot over low heat. Gently add the cod fillets and poach them for about 6 minutes or until the fish is completely opaque. Using a slotted spoon, carefully remove the fish to a plate lined with paper towels. Sprinkle with lemon zest, salt, and pepper. Drizzle with lemon juice and serve immediately.

Nutrition Info:

- Per Serving: Calories: 292;Fat: 34g;Protein: 18g;Carbs: 1g.

Hazelnut Crusted Sea Bass

Servings:2 | Cooking Time: 15 Minutes

Ingredients:

- 2 tablespoons almond butter
- 2 sea bass fillets
- ⅓ cup roasted hazelnuts
- A pinch of cayenne pepper

Directions:

1. Preheat the oven to 425°F. Line a baking dish with waxed paper.
2. Brush the almond butter over the fillets.
3. Pulse the hazelnuts and cayenne in a food processor. Coat the sea bass with the hazelnut mixture, then transfer to the baking dish.
4. Bake in the preheated oven for about 15 minutes. Cool for 5 minutes before serving.

Nutrition Info:

- Per Serving: Calories: 468;Fat: 30.8g;Protein: 40.0g;Carbs: 8.8g.

Parchment Orange & Dill Salmon

Servings:4 | Cooking Time:25 Minutes

Ingredients:

- 2 tbsp butter, melted
- 4 salmon fillets
- Salt and black pepper to taste
- 1 orange, juiced and zested
- 4 tbsp fresh dill, chopped

Directions:

1. Preheat oven to 375 °F. Coat the salmon fillets on both sides with butter. Season with salt and pepper and divide them between 4 pieces of parchment paper. Drizzle the orange juice over each piece of fish and top with orange zest and dill. Wrap the paper around the fish to make packets. Place on a baking sheet and bake for 15-20 minutes until the cod is cooked through. Serve and enjoy!

Nutrition Info:

- Per Serving: Calories: 481;Fat: 21g;Protein: 65g;Carbs: 4.2g.

North African Grilled Fish Fillets

Servings:4 | Cooking Time:15 Minutes

Ingredients:

- 1 tbsp olive oil
- 1 tsp harissa seasoning
- 4 fish fillets
- 2 lemons, sliced
- 2 tbsp lemon juice
- Salt and black pepper to taste

Directions:

1. Preheat your grill to 400 °F. In a bowl, whisk the lemon juice, olive oil, harissa seasoning, salt, and pepper. Coat both sides of the fish with the mixture. Carefully place the lemon slices on the grill, arranging 3-4 slices together in the shape of a fish fillet, and repeat with the remaining slices. Place the fish fillets directly on top of the lemon slices and grill with the lid closed. Turn the fish halfway through the cooking time only if the fillets are more than half an inch thick. The fish is done and ready to serve when it just begins to separate into chunks when pressed gently with a fork. Serve and enjoy!

Nutrition Info:

- Per Serving: Calories: 208;Fat: 12g;Protein: 21g;Carbs: 2g.

Vegetable Mains And Meatless Recipes

Vegetable Mains And Meatless Recipes

Quick Steamed Broccoli

Servings:2 | Cooking Time: 0 Minutes

Ingredients:

- ¼ cup water
- 3 cups broccoli florets
- Salt and ground black pepper, to taste

Directions:

1. Pour the water into the Instant Pot and insert a steamer basket. Place the broccoli florets in the basket.
2. Secure the lid. Select the Manual mode and set the cooking time for 0 minutes at High Pressure.
3. Once cooking is complete, do a quick pressure release. Carefully open the lid.
4. Transfer the broccoli florets to a bowl with cold water to keep bright green color.
5. Season the broccoli with salt and pepper to taste, then serve.

Nutrition Info:

- Per Serving: Calories: 16;Fat: 0.2g;Protein: 1.9g;Carbs: 1.7g.

Baked Honey Acorn Squash

Servings:4 | Cooking Time:35 Minutes

Ingredients:

- 1 acorn squash, cut into wedges
- 2 tbsp olive oil
- 2 tbsp honey
- 2 tbsp rosemary, chopped
- 2 tbsp walnuts, chopped

Directions:

1. Preheat oven to 400°F. In a bowl, mix honey, rosemary, and olive oil. Lay the squash wedges on a baking sheet and drizzle with the honey mixture. Bake for 30 minutes until squash is tender and slightly caramelized, turning each slice over halfway through. Serve cooled sprinkled with walnuts.

Nutrition Info:

- Per Serving: Calories: 136;Fat: 6g;Protein: 0.9g;Carbs: 20g.

Simple Broccoli With Yogurt Sauce

Servings:4 | Cooking Time:25 Minutes

Ingredients:

- 2 tbsp olive oil
- 1 head broccoli, cut into florets
- 2 garlic cloves, minced
- ½ cup Greek yogurt
- Salt and black pepper to taste
- 2 tsp fresh dill, chopped

Directions:

1. Warm olive oil in a pan over medium heat and sauté broccoli, salt, and pepper for 12 minutes. Mix Greek yogurt, dill, and garlic in a small bowl. Drizzle the broccoli with the sauce.

Nutrition Info:

- Per Serving: Calories: 104;Fat: 7.7g;Protein: 4.5g;Carbs: 6g.

Garlic-butter Asparagus With Parmesan

Servings:2 | Cooking Time: 8 Minutes

Ingredients:

- 1 cup water
- 1 pound asparagus, trimmed
- 2 cloves garlic, chopped
- 3 tablespoons almond butter
- Salt and ground black pepper, to taste
- 3 tablespoons grated Parmesan cheese

Directions:

1. Pour the water into the Instant Pot and insert a trivet.
2. Put the asparagus on a tin foil add the butter and garlic. Season to taste with salt and pepper.
3. Fold over the foil and seal the asparagus inside so the foil doesn't come open. Arrange the asparagus on the trivet.
4. Secure the lid. Select the Manual mode and set the cooking time for 8 minutes at High Pressure.
5. Once cooking is complete, do a quick pressure release. Carefully open the lid.
6. Unwrap the foil packet and serve sprinkled with the Parmesan cheese.

Nutrition Info:

- Per Serving: Calories: 243;Fat: 15.7g;Protein: 12.3g;Carbs: 15.3g.

Stuffed Portobello Mushrooms With Spinach

Servings:4 | Cooking Time: 20 Minutes

Ingredients:

- 8 large portobello mushrooms, stems removed
- 3 teaspoons extra-virgin olive oil, divided
- 1 medium red bell pepper, diced
- 4 cups fresh spinach
- ¼ cup crumbled feta cheese

Directions:

1. Preheat the oven to 450ºF.
2. Using a spoon to scoop out the gills of the mushrooms and discard them. Brush the mushrooms with 2 teaspoons of olive oil.
3. Arrange the mushrooms (cap-side down) on a baking sheet. Roast in the preheated oven for 20 minutes.
4. Meantime, in a medium skillet, heat the remaining olive oil over medium heat until it shimmers.
5. Add the bell pepper and spinach and sauté for 8 to 10 minutes, stirring occasionally, or until the spinach is wilted.
6. Remove the mushrooms from the oven to a paper towel-lined plate. Using a spoon to stuff each mushroom with the bell pepper and spinach mixture. Scatter the feta cheese all over.
7. Serve immediately.

Nutrition Info:

- Per Serving: Calories: 115;Fat: 5.9g;Protein: 7.2g;Carbs: 11.5g.

Tradicional Matchuba Green Beans

Servings:4 | Cooking Time:15 Minutes

Ingredients:

- 1 ¼ lb narrow green beans, trimmed
- 3 tbsp butter, melted
- 1 cup Moroccan matbucha
- 2 green onions, chopped
- Salt and black pepper to taste

Directions:

1. Steam the green beans in a pot for 5-6 minutes until tender. Remove to a bowl, reserving the cooking liquid. In a skillet over medium heat, melt the butter. Add in green onions, salt, and black pepper and cook until fragrant. Lower the heat and put in the green beans along with some of the reserved water. Simmer for 3-4 minutes. Serve the green beans with the Sabra Moroccan matbucha as a dip.

Nutrition Info:

- Per Serving: Calories: 125;Fat: 8.6g;Protein: 2.2g;Carbs: 9g.

Parmesan Stuffed Zucchini Boats

Servings:4 | Cooking Time: 15 Minutes

Ingredients:

- 1 cup canned low-sodium chickpeas, drained and rinsed
- 1 cup no-sugar-added spaghetti sauce
- 2 zucchinis
- ¼ cup shredded Parmesan cheese

Directions:

1. Preheat the oven to 425°F.
2. In a medium bowl, stir together the chickpeas and spaghetti sauce.
3. Cut the zucchini in half lengthwise and scrape a spoon gently down the length of each half to remove the seeds.
4. Fill each zucchini half with the chickpea sauce and top with one-quarter of the Parmesan cheese.
5. Place the zucchini halves on a baking sheet and roast in the oven for 15 minutes.
6. Transfer to a plate. Let rest for 5 minutes before serving.

Nutrition Info:

- Per Serving: Calories: 139;Fat: 4.0g;Protein: 8.0g;Carbs: 20.0g.

Minty Broccoli & Walnuts

Servings:2 | Cooking Time:10 Minutes

Ingredients:

- 1 garlic clove, minced
- ½ cups walnuts, chopped
- 3 cups broccoli florets, steamed
- 1 tbsp mint, chopped
- ½ lemon, juiced
- Salt and black pepper to taste

Directions:

1. Mix walnuts, broccoli, garlic, mint, lemon juice, salt, and pepper in a bowl. Serve chilled.

Nutrition Info:

- Per Serving: Calories: 210;Fat: 7g;Protein: 4g;Carbs: 9g.

Roasted Asparagus With Hazelnuts

Servings:4 | Cooking Time:25 Minutes

Ingredients:

- 2 tbsp olive oil
- 1 lb asparagus, trimmed
- ¼ cup hazelnuts, chopped
- 1 lemon, juiced and zested
- Salt and black pepper to taste
- ½ tsp red pepper flakes

Directions:

1. Preheat oven to 425°F. Arrange the asparagus on a baking sheet. Combine olive oil, lemon zest, lemon juice, salt, hazelnuts, and black pepper in a bowl and mix well. Pour the mixture over the asparagus. Place in the oven and roast for 15-20 minutes until tender and lightly charred. Serve topped with red pepper flakes.

Nutrition Info:

- Per Serving: Calories: 112;Fat: 10g;Protein: 3.2g;Carbs: 5.2g.

Baby Kale And Cabbage Salad

Servings:6 | Cooking Time: 0 Minutes

Ingredients:

- 2 bunches baby kale, thinly sliced
- ½ head green savoy cabbage, cored and thinly sliced
- 1 medium red bell pepper, thinly sliced
- 1 garlic clove, thinly sliced
- 1 cup toasted peanuts
- Dressing:
- Juice of 1 lemon
- ¼ cup apple cider vinegar
- 1 teaspoon ground cumin
- ¼ teaspoon smoked paprika

Directions:

1. In a large mixing bowl, toss together the kale and cabbage.
2. Make the dressing: Whisk together the lemon juice, vinegar, cumin and paprika in a small bowl.
3. Pour the dressing over the greens and gently massage with your hands.
4. Add the pepper, garlic and peanuts to the mixing bowl. Toss to combine.
5. Serve immediately.

Nutrition Info:

- Per Serving: Calories: 199;Fat: 12.0g;Protein: 10.0g;Carbs: 17.0g.

Spicy Potato Wedges

Servings:4 | Cooking Time:30 Minutes

Ingredients:
- 1 ½ lb potatoes, peeled and cut into wedges
- 3 tbsp olive oil
- 1 tbsp minced fresh rosemary
- 2 tsp chili powder
- 3 garlic cloves, minced
- Salt and black pepper to taste

Directions:
1. Preheat the oven to 370ºF. Toss the wedges with olive oil, garlic, salt, and pepper. Spread out in a roasting sheet. Roast for 15-20 minutes until browned and crisp at the edges. Remove and sprinkle with chili powder and rosemary.

Nutrition Info:
- Per Serving: Calories: 152;Fat: 7g;Protein: 2.5g;Carbs: 21g.

Sautéed Mushrooms With Garlic & Parsley

Servings:6 | Cooking Time:15 Minutes

Ingredients:
- 3 tbsp butter
- 2 lb cremini mushrooms, sliced
- 2 tbsp garlic, minced
- Salt and black pepper to taste
- 1 tbsp fresh parsley, chopped

Directions:
1. Melt the butter in a skillet over medium heat. Cook the garlic for 1-2 minutes until soft. Stir in the mushrooms and season with salt. Sauté for 7-8 minutes, stirring often. Remove to a serving dish. Top with pepper and parsley to serve.

Nutrition Info:
- Per Serving: Calories: 183;Fat: 9g;Protein: 8.9g;Carbs: 10.1g.

Garlicky Broccoli Rabe

Servings:4 | Cooking Time: 5 To 6 Minutes

Ingredients:

- 14 ounces broccoli rabe, trimmed and cut into 1-inch pieces
- 2 teaspoons salt, plus more for seasoning
- Black pepper, to taste
- 2 tablespoons extra-virgin olive oil
- 3 garlic cloves, minced
- ¼ teaspoon red pepper flakes

Directions:

1. Bring 3 quarts water to a boil in a large saucepan. Add the broccoli rabe and 2 teaspoons of the salt to the boiling water and cook for 2 to 3 minutes, or until wilted and tender.
2. Drain the broccoli rabe. Transfer to ice water and let sit until chilled. Drain again and pat dry.
3. In a skillet over medium heat, heat the oil and add the garlic and red pepper flakes. Sauté for about 2 minutes, or until the garlic begins to sizzle.
4. Increase the heat to medium-high. Stir in the broccoli rabe and cook for about 1 minute, or until heated through, stirring constantly. Season with salt and pepper.
5. Serve immediately.

Nutrition Info:

- Per Serving: Calories: 87;Fat: 7.3g;Protein: 3.4g;Carbs: 4.0g.

Wilted Dandelion Greens With Sweet Onion

Servings:4 | Cooking Time: 15 Minutes

Ingredients:

- 1 tablespoon extra-virgin olive oil
- 2 garlic cloves, minced
- 1 Vidalia onion, thinly sliced
- ½ cup low-sodium vegetable broth
- 2 bunches dandelion greens, roughly chopped
- Freshly ground black pepper, to taste

Directions:

1. Heat the olive oil in a large skillet over low heat.
2. Add the garlic and onion and cook for 2 to 3 minutes, stirring occasionally, or until the onion is translucent.
3. Fold in the vegetable broth and dandelion greens and cook for 5 to 7 minutes until wilted, stirring frequently.
4. Sprinkle with the black pepper and serve on a plate while warm.

Nutrition Info:

- Per Serving: Calories: 81;Fat: 3.9g;Protein: 3.2g;Carbs: 10.8g.

Grilled Za´atar Zucchini Rounds

Servings:4 | Cooking Time:20 Minutes

Ingredients:

- 2 tbsp olive oil
- 4 zucchinis, sliced
- 1 tbsp za'atar seasoning
- Salt to taste
- 2 tbsp parsley, chopped

Directions:

1. Preheat the grill on high. Cut the zucchini lengthways into ½-inch thin pieces. Brush the zucchini 'steaks' with olive oil and season with salt and za'atar seasoning. Grill for 6 minutes on both sides. Sprinkle with parsley and serve.

Nutrition Info:

- Per Serving: Calories: 91;Fat: 7.4g;Protein: 2.4g;Carbs: 6.6g.

5-ingredient Zucchini Fritters

Servings:14 | Cooking Time: 5 Minutes

Ingredients:

- 4 cups grated zucchini
- Salt, to taste
- 2 large eggs, lightly beaten
- ⅓ cup sliced scallions (green and white parts)
- ⅔ all-purpose flour
- ⅛ teaspoon black pepper
- 2 tablespoons olive oil

Directions:

1. Put the grated zucchini in a colander and lightly season with salt. Set aside to rest for 10 minutes. Squeeze out as much liquid from the grated zucchini as possible.
2. Pour the grated zucchini into a bowl. Fold in the beaten eggs, scallions, flour, salt, and pepper and stir until everything is well combined.
3. Heat the olive oil in a large skillet over medium heat until hot.
4. Drop 3 tablespoons mounds of the zucchini mixture onto the hot skillet to make each fritter, pressing them lightly into rounds and spacing them about 2 inches apart.
5. Cook for 2 to 3 minutes. Flip the zucchini fritters and cook for 2 minutes more, or until they are golden brown and cooked through.
6. Remove from the heat to a plate lined with paper towels. Repeat with the remaining zucchini mixture.
7. Serve hot.

Nutrition Info:

- Per Serving: Calories: 113;Fat: 6.1g;Protein: 4.0g;Carbs: 12.2g.

Cauliflower Rice Risotto With Mushrooms

Servings:4 | Cooking Time: 10 Minutes

Ingredients:

- 1 teaspoon extra-virgin olive oil
- ½ cup chopped portobello mushrooms
- 4 cups cauliflower rice
- ½ cup half-and-half
- ¼ cup low-sodium vegetable broth
- 1 cup shredded Parmesan cheese

Directions:

1. In a medium skillet, heat the olive oil over medium-low heat until shimmering.
2. Add the mushrooms and stir-fry for 3 minutes.
3. Stir in the cauliflower rice, half-and-half, and vegetable broth. Cover and bring to a boil over high heat for 5 minutes, stirring occasionally.
4. Add the Parmesan cheese and stir to combine. Continue cooking for an additional 3 minutes until the cheese is melted.
5. Divide the mixture into four bowls and serve warm.

Nutrition Info:

- Per Serving: Calories: 167;Fat: 10.7g;Protein: 12.1g;Carbs: 8.1g.

Balsamic Cherry Tomatoes

Servings:4 | Cooking Time:10 Minutes

Ingredients:

- 2 tbsp olive oil
- 2 lb cherry tomatoes, halved
- 2 tbsp balsamic glaze
- Salt and black pepper to taste
- 1 garlic clove, minced
- 2 tbsp fresh basil, torn

Directions:

1. Warm the olive oil in a skillet over medium heat. Add the cherry tomatoes and cook for 1-2 minutes, stirring occasionally. Stir in garlic, salt, and pepper and cook until fragrant, about 30 seconds. Drizzle with balsamic glaze and decorate with basil. Serve and enjoy!

Nutrition Info:

- Per Serving: Calories: 45;Fat: 2.5g;Protein: 1.1g;Carbs: 5.6g.

Pea & Carrot Noodles

Servings:4 | Cooking Time:25 Minutes

Ingredients:

- 2 tbsp olive oil
- 4 carrots, spiralized
- 1 sweet onion, chopped
- 2 cups peas
- 2 garlic cloves, minced
- ¼ cup chopped fresh parsley
- Salt and black pepper to taste

Directions:

1. Warm 2 tbsp of olive oil in a pot over medium heat and sauté the onion and garlic for 3 minutes until just tender and fragrant. Add in spiralized carrots and cook for 4 minutes. Mix in peas, salt, and pepper and cook for 4 minutes. Drizzle with the remaining olive oil and sprinkle with parsley.

Nutrition Info:

- Per Serving: Calories: 157;Fat: 7g;Protein: 4.8g;Carbs: 19.6g.

Simple Zoodles

Servings:2 | Cooking Time: 5 Minutes

Ingredients:

- 2 tablespoons avocado oil
- 2 medium zucchinis, spiralized
- ¼ teaspoon salt
- Freshly ground black pepper, to taste

Directions:

1. Heat the avocado oil in a large skillet over medium heat until it shimmers.
2. Add the zucchini noodles, salt, and black pepper to the skillet and toss to coat. Cook for 1 to 2 minutes, stirring constantly, until tender.
3. Serve warm.

Nutrition Info:

- Per Serving: Calories: 128;Fat: 14.0g;Protein: 0.3g;Carbs: 0.3g.

Sides , Salads, And Soups Recipes

Sides , Salads, And Soups Recipes

Parsley Carrot & Cabbage Salad

Servings:4 | Cooking Time:10 Minutes

Ingredients:

- 2 tbsp olive oil
- 1 green cabbage head, torn
- 1 tbsp lemon juice
- 1 carrot, grated
- Salt and black pepper to taste
- ¼ cup parsley, chopped

Directions:

1. Mix olive oil, lemon juice, carrot, parsley, salt, pepper, and cabbage in a bowl. Serve right away.

Nutrition Info:

- Per Serving: Calories: 110;Fat: 5g;Protein: 5g;Carbs: 5g.

Tasty Cucumber & Couscous Salad

Servings:4 | Cooking Time:30 Minutes

Ingredients:

- ¼ cup olive oil
- 2 tbsp balsamic vinegar
- 1 cup couscous
- 1 cucumber, sliced
- Salt and black pepper to taste
- 2 tbsp lemon juice

Directions:

1. Place couscous in a bowl with 3 cups of hot water and let sit for 10 minutes. Fluff with a fork and remove to a bowl. Stir in cucumber, salt, pepper, lemon juice, vinegar, and olive oil. Serve immediately.

Nutrition Info:

- Per Serving: Calories: 180;Fat: 6g;Protein: 5g;Carbs: 12g.

Balsamic Carrots With Feta Cheese

Servings:4 | Cooking Time:40 Minutes

Ingredients:

- 2 tbsp olive oil
- 1 pound baby carrots
- 3 tbsp balsamic vinegar
- ½ cup feta cheese, crumbled
- ½ red chili, sliced
- Salt and black pepper to taste

Directions:

1. Preheat oven to 425° F. Combine carrots, salt, olive oil, and pepper in a bowl. Arrange them on a baking tray and drizzle with honey; cook for 25-30 minutes until the carrots are golden. Mix the carrots with vinegar and top with feta.

Nutrition Info:

- Per Serving: Calories: 152;Fat: 11g;Protein: 3.4g;Carbs: 10g.

Greek Chicken, Tomato, And Olive Salad

Servings:2 | Cooking Time: 0 Minutes

Ingredients:

- Salad:
- 2 grilled boneless, skinless chicken breasts, sliced
- 10 cherry tomatoes, halved
- 8 pitted Kalamata olives, halved
- ½ cup thinly sliced red onion
- Dressing:
- ¼ cup balsamic vinegar
- 1 teaspoon freshly squeezed lemon juice
- ¼ teaspoon sea salt
- ¼ teaspoon freshly ground black pepper
- 2 teaspoons extra-virgin olive oil
- For Serving:
- 2 cups roughly chopped romaine lettuce
- ½ cup crumbled feta cheese

Directions:

1. Combine the ingredients for the salad in a large bowl. Toss to combine well.
2. Combine the ingredients for the dressing in a small bowl. Stir to mix well.
3. Pour the dressing the bowl of salad, then toss to coat well. Wrap the bowl in plastic and refrigerate for at least 2 hours.
4. Remove the bowl from the refrigerator. Spread the lettuce on a large plate, then top with marinated salad. Scatter the salad with feta cheese and serve immediately.

Nutrition Info:

- Per Serving: Calories: 328;Fat: 16.9g;Protein: 27.6g;Carbs: 15.9g.

Green Beans With Tahini-lemon Sauce

Servings:2 | Cooking Time: 10 Minutes

Ingredients:

- 1 pound green beans, washed and trimmed
- 2 tablespoons tahini
- 1 garlic clove, minced
- Grated zest and juice of 1 lemon
- Salt and black pepper, to taste
- 1 teaspoon toasted black or white sesame seeds (optional)

Directions:

1. Steam the beans in a medium saucepan fitted with a steamer basket (or by adding ¼ cup water to a covered saucepan) over medium-high heat. Drain, reserving the cooking water.
2. Mix the tahini, garlic, lemon zest and juice, and salt and pepper to taste. Use the reserved cooking water to thin the sauce as desired.
3. Toss the green beans with the sauce and garnish with the sesame seeds, if desired. Serve immediately.

Nutrition Info:

- Per Serving: Calories: 188;Fat: 8.4g;Protein: 7.2g;Carbs: 22.2g.

Zesty Asparagus Salad

Servings:4 | Cooking Time:10 Minutes

Ingredients:

- 4 tbsp olive oil
- 1 lb asparagus
- 1 garlic clove, minced
- Salt and black pepper to taste
- 1 tbsp balsamic vinegar
- 1 tbsp lemon zest

Directions:

1. Roast the asparagus in a greased skillet over medium heat for 5-6 minutes, turning once. Season to taste. Toss with garlic, olive oil, lemon zest, and vinegar. Serve.

Nutrition Info:

- Per Serving: Calories: 148;Fat: 13.6g;Protein: 3g;Carbs: 5.7g.

Lemony Yogurt Sauce

Servings:4 | Cooking Time:5 Minutes

Ingredients:

- 1 cup plain yogurt
- 1 tbsp fresh chives, chopped
- ½ lemon, zested and juiced
- 1 garlic clove, minced
- Salt and black pepper to taste

Directions:

1. Place the yogurt, lemon zest and juice, and garlic in a bowl and mix well. Season with salt and pepper. Let sit for about 30 minutes to blend the flavors. Store in an airtight container in the refrigerator for up to 2-3 days. Serve topped with chives.

Nutrition Info:

- Per Serving: Calories: 258;Fat: 8g;Protein: 8.9g;Carbs: 12.9g.

Garlic Herb Butter

Servings:4 | Cooking Time:5 Minutes

Ingredients:

- ½ cup butter, softened
- 1 garlic clove, finely minced
- 2 tsp fresh rosemary, chopped
- 1 tsp marjoram, chopped
- Salt to taste

Directions:

1. Blend the butter, garlic, rosemary, marjoram, and salt in your food processor until the mixture is well combined, smooth, and creamy, scraping down the sides as necessary. Scrape the butter mixture with a spatula into a glass container and cover. Store in the refrigerator for up to 30 days.

Nutrition Info:

- Per Serving: Calories: 103;Fat: 12.4g;Protein: 0g;Carbs: 0g.

Easy Roasted Cauliflower

Servings:2 | Cooking Time: 20 Minutes

Ingredients:

- ½ large head cauliflower, stemmed and broken into florets
- 1 tablespoon olive oil
- 2 tablespoons freshly squeezed lemon juice
- 2 tablespoons tahini
- 1 teaspoon harissa paste
- Pinch salt

Directions:

1. Preheat the oven to 400°F. Line a sheet pan with parchment paper.
2. Toss the cauliflower florets with the olive oil in a large bowl and transfer to the sheet pan.
3. Roast in the preheated oven for 15 minutes, flipping the cauliflower once or twice, or until it starts to become golden.
4. Meanwhile, in a separate bowl, combine the lemon juice, tahini, harissa, and salt and stir to mix well.
5. Remove the pan from the oven and toss the cauliflower with the lemon tahini sauce. Return to the oven and roast for another 5 minutes. Serve hot.

Nutrition Info:

- Per Serving: Calories: 205;Fat: 15.0g;Protein: 4.0g;Carbs: 15.0g.

Creamy Tomato Hummus Soup

Servings:4 | Cooking Time:10 Minutes

Ingredients:

- 1 can diced tomatoes
- 1 cup traditional hummus
- 4 cups chicken stock
- ¼ cup basil leaves, sliced
- 1 cup garlic croutons

Directions:

1. Place the tomatoes, hummus, and chicken stock in your blender and blend until smooth. Pour the mixture into a saucepan over medium heat and bring it to a boil. Pour the soup into bowls. Sprinkle with basil and serve with croutons.

Nutrition Info:

- Per Serving: Calories: 148;Fat: 6.2g;Protein: 5g;Carbs: 18.8g.

Orange-honey Glazed Carrots

Servings:2 | Cooking Time: 15 To 20 Minutes

Ingredients:

- ½ pound rainbow carrots, peeled
- 2 tablespoons fresh orange juice
- 1 tablespoon honey
- ½ teaspoon coriander
- Pinch salt

Directions:

1. Preheat the oven to 400°F.
2. Cut the carrots lengthwise into slices of even thickness and place in a large bowl.
3. Stir together the orange juice, honey, coriander, and salt in a small bowl. Pour the orange juice mixture over the carrots and toss until well coated.
4. Spread the carrots in a baking dish in a single layer. Roast for 15 to 20 minutes until fork-tender.
5. Let cool for 5 minutes before serving.

Nutrition Info:

- Per Serving: Calories: 85;Fat: 0g;Protein: 1.0g;Carbs: 21.0g.

Herby Yogurt Sauce

Servings:4 | Cooking Time:5 Minutes

Ingredients:

- ¼ tsp fresh lemon juice
- 1 cup plain yogurt
- 2 tbsp fresh cilantro, minced
- 2 tbsp fresh mint, minced
- 1 garlic clove, minced
- Salt and black pepper to taste

Directions:

1. Place the lemon juice, yogurt, cilantro, mint, and garlic together in a bowl and mix well. Season with salt and pepper. Let sit for about 30 minutes to blend the flavors. Store in an airtight container in the refrigerator for up to 2-3 days.

Nutrition Info:

- Per Serving: Calories: 46;Fat: 0.8g;Protein: 3.6g;Carbs: 4.8g.

Simple Tahini Sauce

Servings:4 | Cooking Time:5 Minutes

Ingredients:

- ¼ tsp ground cumin
- ½ cup tahini
- ¼ cup lemon juice
- 2 garlic cloves, minced
- Salt and black pepper to taste
- 1 tbsp parsley, chopped

Directions:

1. Place the tahini, lemon juice, and garlic, ½ cup of water in a bowl and whisk until combined. Season with salt and pepper to taste. Let sit for about 30 minutes until flavors meld. Refrigerate for up to 3 days. Serve topped with parsley.

Nutrition Info:

- Per Serving: Calories: 306;Fat: 13.3g;Protein: 2g;Carbs: 3.2g.

Homemade Herbes De Provence Spice

Servings:4 | Cooking Time:5 Minutes

Ingredients:

- 2 tbsp dried oregano
- 2 tbsp dried thyme
- 2 tbsp dried marjoram
- 2 tbsp dried rosemary
- 2 tsp fennel seeds, toasted

Directions:

1. Mix the oregano, thyme, marjoram, rosemary, and fennel seeds in a bowl. Store the spices in an airtight container at room temperature for up to 7-9 months.

Nutrition Info:

- Per Serving: Calories: 32;Fat: 1.1g;Protein: 1.4g;Carbs: 6.0g.

Cherry, Plum, Artichoke, And Cheese Board

Servings:4 | Cooking Time: 0 Minutes

Ingredients:

- 2 cups rinsed cherries
- 2 cups rinsed and sliced plums
- 2 cups rinsed carrots, cut into sticks
- 1 cup canned low-sodium artichoke hearts, rinsed and drained
- 1 cup cubed feta cheese

Directions:

1. Arrange all the ingredients in separated portions on a clean board or a large tray, then serve with spoons, knife, and forks.

Nutrition Info:

- Per Serving: Calories: 417;Fat: 13.8g;Protein: 20.1g;Carbs: 56.2g.

Asparagus & Red Onion Side Dish

Servings:6 | Cooking Time:20 Minutes

Ingredients:

- 2 tbsp olive oil
- 1 ½ lb asparagus spears
- 1 tsp garlic powder
- 1 red onion, sliced
- Salt and black pepper to taste

Directions:

1. Preheat oven to 390° F. Brush the asparagus with olive oil. Toss with garlic powder, salt, and black pepper. Roast in the oven for about 15 minutes. Top the roasted asparagus with the red onion. Serve and enjoy!

Nutrition Info:

- Per Serving: Calories: 129;Fat: 3g;Protein: 3g;Carbs: 7g.

Greek Tahini Sauce

Servings:4 | Cooking Time:5 Minutes

Ingredients:

- ¼ tsp dill, chopped
- ⅓ cup tahini
- ⅓ cup Greek yogurt
- 3 tbsp lemon juice
- 1 garlic clove, minced
- Salt to taste

Directions:

1. Place the dill, tahini, yogurt, lemon juice, garlic, salt, ¼ cup of water in a bowl and mix to combine. Let sit for about 30 minutes to blend the flavors. Store in an airtight container in the refrigerator for up to 2-3 days.

Nutrition Info:

- Per Serving: Calories: 407;Fat: 8g;Protein: 3.6g;Carbs: 2.7g.

Roasted Cherry Tomato & Fennel

Servings:4 | Cooking Time:35 Minutes

Ingredients:

- ¼ cup olive oil
- 20 cherry tomatoes, halved
- 2 fennel bulbs, cut into wedges
- 10 black olives, sliced
- 1 lemon, cut into wedges
- Salt and black pepper to taste

Directions:

1. Preheat oven to 425° F. Combine fennel, olive oil, tomatoes, salt, and pepper in a bowl. Place in a baking pan and roast in the oven for about 25 minutes until golden. Top with olives and serve with lemon wedges on the side.

Nutrition Info:

- Per Serving: Calories: 268;Fat: 15.2g;Protein: 7g;Carbs: 33g.

Balsamic Watermelon & Feta Salad

Servings:2 | Cooking Time:10 Minutes

Ingredients:

- 3 cups packed arugula
- 2 ½ cups watermelon, cubed
- 2 oz feta cheese, crumbled
- 2 tbsp balsamic glaze
- 1 tsp mint leaves, chopped

Directions:

1. Place the arugula on a salad plate. Top with watermelon cubes and sprinkle with feta cheese. Drizzle the balsamic glaze all over and garnish with chopped mint leaves. Serve.

Nutrition Info:

- Per Serving: Calories: 159;Fat: 7.2g;Protein: 6.1g;Carbs: 21g.

Arugula, Watermelon, And Feta Salad

Servings:2 | Cooking Time: 0 Minutes

Ingredients:

- 3 cups packed arugula
- 2½ cups watermelon, cut into bite-size cubes
- 2 ounces feta cheese, crumbled
- 2 tablespoons balsamic glaze

Directions:

1. Divide the arugula between two plates.
2. Divide the watermelon cubes between the beds of arugula.
3. Scatter half of the feta cheese over each salad.
4. Drizzle about 1 tablespoon of the glaze (or more if desired) over each salad. Serve immediately.

Nutrition Info:

- Per Serving: Calories: 157;Fat: 6.9g;Protein: 6.1g;Carbs: 22.0g.

Classic Potato Salad With Green Onions

Servings:4 | Cooking Time:25 Minutes

Ingredients:

- 2 ½ lb baby potatoes, halved
- Salt and black pepper to taste
- 1 cup light mayonnaise
- Juice of 1 lemon
- 2 green onions, chopped
- ¼ cup parsley, chopped

Directions:

1. Place potatoes and enough water in a pot over medium heat and bring to a boil. Cook for 12 minutes and drain; set aside.
2. In a bowl, mix mayonnaise, salt, pepper, lemon juice, and green onions. Add in the baby potatoes and toss to coat. Top with parsley and serve immediately.

Nutrition Info:

- Per Serving: Calories: 360;Fat: 20g;Protein: 11g;Carbs: 25g.

Quick Za´atar Spice

Servings:4 | Cooking Time:5 Minutes

Ingredients:

- 1 tsp ground cumin
- 1 tsp ground coriander
- ½ cup dried thyme
- 2 tbsp sesame seeds, toasted
- 1 ½ tbsp ground sumac
- ¼ tsp Aleppo chili flakes

Directions:

1. Mix all the ingredients in a bowl. Store in a glass jar at room temperature for up to 7-9 months.

Nutrition Info:

- Per Serving: Calories: 175;Fat: 13.9g;Protein: 5g;Carbs: 12g.

Balsamic Roasted Mushrooms

Servings:6 | Cooking Time:30 Min + Marinating Time

Ingredients:

- 6 portobello mushroom caps
- 1 tsp extra-virgin olive oil
- 2 tsp balsamic vinegar
- Salt and garlic powder to taste
- ¼ cup fresh thyme, chopped
- ¼ cup fresh oregano, chopped

Directions:

1. Mix together all the ingredients, except for the mushrooms, in a large bowl. Add in the mushroom caps, cover with lid, and refrigerate for at least 2 hours at room temperature.
2. Preheat oven to 400° F. Arrange the mushrooms on a parchment-lined baking sheet. Roast them for 15–20 minutes until cooked. To serve, slice the caps into small wedges.

Nutrition Info:

- Per Serving: Calories: 28;Fat: 1g;Protein: 2g;Carbs: 4g.

Spinach & Bell Pepper Salad

Servings:4 | Cooking Time:10 Minutes

Ingredients:

- 10 oz baby spinach
- 1 red bell pepper, sliced
- 2 cups corn
- 1 lemon, zested and juiced
- Salt and black pepper to taste

Directions:

1. Combine bell pepper, corn, lemon juice, lemon zest, baby spinach, salt, and pepper in a bowl. Serve immediately.

Nutrition Info:

- Per Serving: Calories: 190;Fat: 9g;Protein: 2g;Carbs: 6g.

Mascarpone Sweet Potato Mash

Servings:4 | Cooking Time:30 Minutes

Ingredients:

- ¼ cup mascarpone cheese, softened
- ¼ cup olive oil
- ½ tsp ground nutmeg
- 1 ¼ lb sweet potatoes, cubed
- Salt and black pepper to taste
- 1 tbsp fresh chives, chopped

Directions:

1. Place the potatoes in a pot over high heat and cover with water. Bring to a boil, then lower the heat and simmer covered for 20 minutes. Drain the potatoes and back to the pot. Stir in mascarpone, olive oil, nutmeg, salt, and pepper. Mash them with a potato masher until smooth. Sprinkle with chives.

Nutrition Info:

- Per Serving: Calories: 304;Fat: 15g;Protein: 4g;Carbs: 40.2g.

Rosemary Garlic Infused Olive Oil

Servings:4 | Cooking Time:35 Minutes

Ingredients:

- Salt and black pepper to taste
- 1 cup extra-virgin olive oil
- 4 large garlic cloves, smashed
- 4 sprigs rosemary

Directions:

1. Warm the olive oil in a medium skillet over low heat and sauté garlic and rosemary sprigs for 30-40 minutes, until fragrant and garlic is very tender, stirring occasionally. Don't let the oil get too hot, or the garlic will burn and become bitter. Remove from the heat and leave to cool slightly. Using a slotted spoon, remove the garlic and rosemary and pour the oil into a glass container. Use cooled.

Nutrition Info:

- Per Serving: Calories: 241;Fat: 26.8g;Protein: 0g;Carbs: 1.1g.

Cheesy Peach And Walnut Salad

Servings:1 | Cooking Time: 0 Minutes

Ingredients:

- 1 ripe peach, pitted and sliced
- ¼ cup chopped walnuts, toasted
- ¼ cup shredded Parmesan cheese
- 1 teaspoon raw honey
- Zest of 1 lemon
- 1 tablespoon chopped fresh mint

Directions:

1. Combine the peach, walnut, and cheese in a medium bowl, then drizzle with honey. Spread the lemon zest and mint on top. Toss to combine everything well.
2. Serve immediately.

Nutrition Info:

- Per Serving: Calories: 373;Fat: 26.4g;Protein: 12.9g;Carbs: 27.0g.

Cheesy Roasted Broccolini

Servings:2 | Cooking Time: 10 Minutes

Ingredients:

- 1 bunch broccolini
- 1 tablespoon olive oil
- ½ teaspoon garlic powder
- ¼ teaspoon salt
- 2 tablespoons grated Romano cheese

Directions:

1. Preheat the oven to 400ºF. Line a sheet pan with parchment paper.
2. Slice the tough ends off the broccolini and put in a medium bowl. Add the olive oil, garlic powder, and salt and toss to coat well. Arrange the broccolini on the prepared sheet pan.
3. Roast in the preheated oven for 7 minutes, flipping halfway through the cooking time.
4. Remove the pan from the oven and sprinkle the cheese over the broccolini. Using tongs, carefully flip the broccolini over to coat all sides.
5. Return to the oven and cook for an additional 2 to 3 minutes, or until the cheese melts and starts to turn golden. Serve warm.

Nutrition Info:

- Per Serving: Calories: 114;Fat: 9.0g;Protein: 4.0g;Carbs: 5.0g.

Warm Kale Salad With Red Bell Pepper

Servings:4 | Cooking Time:15 Minutes

Ingredients:

- 1 tbsp olive oil
- 4 cups kale, torn
- 2 cloves garlic, minced
- 1 red bell pepper, diced
- Salt and black pepper to taste
- ½ lemon, juiced

Directions:

1. Warm the olive oil in a large skillet over medium heat and add the garlic. Cook for 1 minute, and then add the bell pepper. Cook for 4-5 minutes until the pepper is tender. Stir in the kale. Cook for 3-4 minutes or just until wilted, then remove from heat. Place pepper and kale in a bowl and season with salt and black pepper. Drizzle with lemon juice.

Nutrition Info:

- Per Serving: Calories: 123;Fat: 4g;Protein: 6g;Carbs: 22g.

Mediterranean Tomato Hummus Soup

Servings:2 | Cooking Time: 10 Minutes

Ingredients:

- 1 can crushed tomatoes with basil
- 2 cups low-sodium chicken stock
- 1 cup roasted red pepper hummus
- Salt, to taste
- ¼ cup thinly sliced fresh basil leaves, for garnish (optional)

Directions:

1. Combine the canned tomatoes, hummus, and chicken stock in a blender and blend until smooth. Pour the mixture into a saucepan and bring it to a boil. Season with salt to taste.
2. Serve garnished with the fresh basil, if desired.

Nutrition Info:

- Per Serving: Calories: 147;Fat: 6.2g;Protein: 5.2g;Carbs: 20.1g.

Classic Aioli

Servings:6 | Cooking Time:10 Minutes

Ingredients:

- ½ cup sunseed oil
- 1 garlic clove, minced
- 2 tsp lemon juice
- 1 tsp lemon zest
- 1 large egg yolk
- Salt to taste

Directions:

1. Blitz all the ingredients in a large bowl with an immersion blender until everything is well combined and thick. Store in an airtight container in the refrigerator for up to 2-3 days.

Nutrition Info:

- Per Serving: Calories: 181;Fat: 9.7g;Protein: 3.3g;Carbs: 4g.

Effortless Bell Pepper Salad

Servings:4 | Cooking Time:10 Minutes

Ingredients:

- 2 green bell peppers, cut into thick strips
- 2 red bell peppers, cut into thick strips
- 2 tbsp olive oil
- ½ cup feta cheese, crumbled
- Salt and black pepper to taste

Directions:

1. Combine bell peppers, olive oil, feta cheese, salt, and pepper in a bowl. Serve immediately.

Nutrition Info:

- Per Serving: Calories: 210;Fat: 6g;Protein: 4g;Carbs: 5g.

Pecorino Zucchini Strips

Servings:4 | Cooking Time:30 Minutes

Ingredients:

- 4 zucchini, quartered lengthwise
- 2 tbsp olive oil
- ½ cup grated Pecorino cheese
- 1 tbsp dried dill
- ¼ tsp garlic powder
- Salt and black pepper to taste

Directions:

1. Preheat oven to 350° F. Combine zucchini and olive oil in a bowl. Mix cheese, salt, garlic powder, dill, and pepper in a bowl. Add in zucchini and toss to combine. Arrange the zucchini fingers on a lined baking sheet and bake for about 20 minutes until golden Set oven to broil and broil for 2 minutes until crispy. Serve and enjoy!

Nutrition Info:

- Per Serving: Calories: 103;Fat: 8.2g;Protein: 3.5g;Carbs: 6g.

Balsamic Potato Salad With Capers

Servings:2 | Cooking Time:30 Minutes

Ingredients:

- 2 tbsp olive oil
- 3 potatoes, peeled and cubed
- 2 tbsp capers
- 1 red onion, chopped
- 1 tbsp balsamic vinegar
- Salt and black pepper to taste

Directions:

1. Place potatoes in a pot over medium heat with enough water and bring to a boil; cook for 20 minutes. Drain and remove to a bowl. Stir in red onion, olive oil, capers, vinegar, salt, and pepper. Serve chilled.

Nutrition Info:

- Per Serving: Calories: 210;Fat: 6g;Protein: 5g;Carbs: 12g.

Spinach & Cherry Tomato Salad

Servings:4 | Cooking Time:15 Minutes

Ingredients:

- ¼ cup olive oil
- 4 cups baby spinach leaves
- 10 cherry tomatoes, halved
- Salt and black pepper to taste
- ¼ cup pumpkin seeds
- ½ lemon, juiced

Directions:

1. Toast the pumpkin seeds in a dry sauté pan over medium heat for 2 minutes, shaking often. Let cool. In a small jar, add the olive oil, lemon juice, salt, and pepper. Place the baby spinach on a salad platter and top with cherry tomatoes. Drizzle with the vinaigrette and sprinkle with toasted pumpkin seeds. Serve immediately.

Nutrition Info:

- Per Serving: Calories: 199;Fat: 14g;Protein: 2g;Carbs: 36g.

Cucumber Salad With Goat Cheese

Servings:4 | Cooking Time:15 Minutes

Ingredients:
- 2 tbsp olive oil
- 4 oz goat cheese, crumbled
- 2 cucumbers, sliced
- 2 spring onions, chopped
- 2 garlic cloves, grated
- Salt and black pepper to taste

Directions:
1. Combine cucumbers, spring onions, olive oil, garlic, salt, pepper, and goat cheese in a bowl. Serve chilled.

Nutrition Info:
- Per Serving: Calories: 150;Fat: 6g;Protein: 6g;Carbs: 8g.

Garlic Wilted Greens

Servings:2 | Cooking Time: 5 Minutes

Ingredients:
- 1 tablespoon olive oil
- 2 garlic cloves, minced
- 3 cups sliced greens (spinach, chard, beet greens, dandelion greens, or a combination)
- Pinch salt
- Pinch red pepper flakes (or more to taste)

Directions:
1. Heat the olive oil in a skillet over medium-high heat.
2. Add garlic and sauté for 30 seconds, or just until fragrant.
3. Add the greens, salt, and pepper flakes and stir to combine. Let the greens wilt, but do not overcook.
4. Remove from the skillet and serve on a plate.

Nutrition Info:
- Per Serving: Calories: 93;Fat: 6.8g;Protein: 1.2g;Carbs: 7.3g.

Fruits , Desserts And Snacks Recipes

Fruits , Desserts And Snacks Recipes

Mint-watermelon Gelato

Servings:4 | Cooking Time:10 Min + Freezing Time

Ingredients:

- ¼ cup honey
- 4 cups watermelon cubes
- ¼ cup lemon juice
- 12 mint leaves to serve

Directions:

1. In a food processor, blend the watermelon, honey, and lemon juice to form a purée with chunks. Transfer to a freezer-proof container and place in the freezer for 1 hour.
2. Remove the container from and scrape with a fork. Return the to the freezer and repeat the process every half hour until the sorbet is completely frozen, for around 4 hours. Share into bowls, garnish with mint leaves, and serve.

Nutrition Info:

- Per Serving: Calories: 149;Fat: 0.4g;Protein: 1.8g;Carbs: 38g.

Grilled Pesto Halloumi Cheese

Servings:2 | Cooking Time:9 Minutes

Ingredients:

- 1 tbsp olive oil
- 3 oz Halloumi cheese
- 2 tsp pesto sauce
- 1 tomato, sliced

Directions:

1. Cut the cheese into 2 rectangular pieces. Heat a griddle pan over medium heat. Drizzle the halloumi slices with and add to the pan. After about 2 minutes, check to see if the cheese is golden on the bottom. Flip the slices, top each with pesto, and cook for another 2 minutes, or until the second side is golden. Serve with tomato slices.

Nutrition Info:

- Per Serving: Calories: 177;Fat: 14g;Protein: 10g;Carbs: 4g.

Cantaloupe & Watermelon Balls

Servings:4 | Cooking Time:5 Min + Chilling Time

Ingredients:

- 2 cups watermelon balls
- 2 cups cantaloupe balls
- ½ cup orange juice
- ¼ cup lemon juice
- 1 tbsp orange zest

Directions:

1. Place the watermelon and cantaloupe in a bowl. In another bowl, mix the lemon juice, orange juice and zest. Pour over the fruit. Transfer to the fridge covered for 5 hours. Serve.

Nutrition Info:

- Per Serving: Calories: 71;Fat: 0g;Protein: 1.5g;Carbs: 18g.

Coconut Blueberries With Brown Rice

Servings:4 | Cooking Time: 10 Minutes

Ingredients:

- 1 cup fresh blueberries
- 2 cups unsweetened coconut milk
- 1 teaspoon ground ginger
- ¼ cup maple syrup
- Sea salt, to taste
- 2 cups cooked brown rice

Directions:

1. Put all the ingredients, except for the brown rice, in a pot. Stir to combine well.
2. Cook over medium-high heat for 7 minutes or until the blueberries are tender.
3. Pour in the brown rice and cook for 3 more minute or until the rice is soft. Stir constantly.
4. Serve immediately.

Nutrition Info:

- Per Serving: Calories: 470;Fat: 24.8g;Protein: 6.2g;Carbs: 60.1g.

Dark Chocolate Barks

Servings:6 | Cooking Time:20 Min + Freezing Time

Ingredients:

- ½ cup quinoa
- ½ tsp sea salt
- 1 cup dark chocolate chips
- ½ tsp mint extract
- ½ cup pomegranate seeds

Directions:

1. Toast the quinoa in a greased saucepan for 2-3 minutes, stirring frequently. Remove the pan from the stove and mix in the salt. Set aside 2 tablespoons of the toasted quinoa.
2. Microwave the chocolate for 1 minute. Stir until the chocolate is completely melted. Mix the toasted quinoa and mint extract into the melted chocolate. Line a large, rimmed baking sheet with parchment paper. Spread the chocolate mixture onto the sheet. Sprinkle the remaining 2 tablespoons of quinoa and pomegranate seeds, pressing with a spatula. Freeze the mixture for 10-15 minutes or until set. Remove and break into about 2-inch jagged pieces. Store in the refrigerator until ready to serve.

Nutrition Info:

- Per Serving: Calories: 268;Fat: 12g;Protein: 4g;Carbs: 37g.

Hummus & Tomato Stuffed Cucumbers

Servings:2 | Cooking Time:5 Minutes

Ingredients:

- 1 cucumber, halved lengthwise
- ½ cup hummus
- 5 cherry tomatoes, halved
- 2 tbsp fresh basil, minced

Directions:

1. Using a paring knife, scoop most of the seeds from the inside of each cucumber piece to make a cup, being careful not to cut all the way through. Fill each cucumber cup with about 1 tablespoon of hummus. Top with cherry tomatoes and basil.

Nutrition Info:

- Per Serving: Calories: 135;Fat: 6g;Protein: 6g;Carbs: 16g.

Chive Ricotta Spread

Servings:4 | Cooking Time:5 Minutes

Ingredients:

- 2 tbsp extra virgin olive oil
- 8 oz ricotta cheese, crumbled
- 2 tbsp fresh parsley, chopped
- ¼ cup chives, chopped
- Salt and black pepper to taste

Directions:

1. In a blender, pulse ricotta cheese, parsley, chives, salt, pepper, and olive oil until smooth. Serve.

Nutrition Info:

- Per Serving: Calories: 260;Fat: 12g;Protein: 12g;Carbs: 9g.

Fruit Skewers With Vanilla Labneh

Servings:4 | Cooking Time:15 Min + Straining Time

Ingredients:

- 2 cups plain yogurt
- 2 tbsp honey
- 1 tsp vanilla extract
- A pinch of salt
- 2 mangoes, cut into chunks

Directions:

1. Place a fine sieve lined with cheesecloth over a bowl and spoon the yogurt into the sieve. Allow the liquid to drain off for 12-24 hours hours. Transfer the strained yogurt to a bowl and mix in the honey, vanilla, and salt. Set it aside.
2. Heat your grill to medium-high. Thread the fruit onto skewers and grill for 2 minutes on each side until the fruit is softened and has grill marks on each side. Serve with labneh.

Nutrition Info:

- Per Serving: Calories: 292;Fat: 6g;Protein: 5g;Carbs: 60g.

Strawberries With Balsamic Vinegar

Servings:2 | Cooking Time: 0 Minutes

Ingredients:

- 2 cups strawberries, hulled and sliced
- 2 tablespoons sugar
- 2 tablespoons balsamic vinegar

Directions:

1. Place the sliced strawberries in a bowl, sprinkle with the sugar, and drizzle lightly with the balsamic vinegar.
2. Toss to combine well and allow to sit for about 10 minutes before serving.

Nutrition Info:

- Per Serving: Calories: 92;Fat: 0.4g;Protein: 1.0g;Carbs: 21.7g.

Wrapped Pears In Prosciutto

Servings:4 | Cooking Time:5 Minutes

Ingredients:

- 2 pears, cored and cut into wedges
- 4 oz prosciutto slices, halved lengthwise
- 1 tbsp chives, chopped
- 1 tsp red pepper flakes

Directions:

1. Wrap the pear wedges with prosciutto slices. Transfer them to a platter. Garnish with chives and pepper flakes. Serve.

Nutrition Info:

- Per Serving: Calories: 35;Fat: 2g;Protein: 12g;Carbs: 5g.

Fruit And Nut Chocolate Bark

Servings:2 | Cooking Time: 2 Minutes

Ingredients:

- 2 tablespoons chopped nuts
- 3 ounces dark chocolate chips
- ¼ cup chopped dried fruit (blueberries, apricots, figs, prunes, or any combination of those)

Directions:

1. Line a sheet pan with parchment paper and set aside.
2. Add the nuts to a skillet over medium-high heat and toast for 60 seconds, or just fragrant. Set aside to cool.
3. Put the chocolate chips in a microwave-safe glass bowl and microwave on High for 1 minute.
4. Stir the chocolate and allow any unmelted chips to warm and melt. If desired, heat for an additional 20 to 30 seconds.
5. Transfer the chocolate to the prepared sheet pan. Scatter the dried fruit and toasted nuts over the chocolate evenly and gently pat in so they stick.
6. Place the sheet pan in the refrigerator for at least 1 hour to let the chocolate harden.
7. When ready, break into pieces and serve.

Nutrition Info:

- Per Serving: Calories: 285;Fat: 16.1g;Protein: 4.0g;Carbs: 38.7g.

5-minute Avocado Spread

Servings:4 | Cooking Time:5 Minutes

Ingredients:

- 2 avocados, chopped
- ½ cup heavy cream
- 1 serrano pepper, chopped
- Salt and black pepper to taste
- 2 tbsp cilantro, chopped
- ¼ cup lime juice

Directions:

1. In a food processor, blitz heavy cream, serrano pepper, salt, pepper, avocados, cilantro, and lime juice until smooth. Refrigerate before serving.

Nutrition Info:

- Per Serving: Calories: 210;Fat: 15g;Protein: 8g;Carbs: 9g.

Kid´s Marzipan Balls

Servings:6 | Cooking Time:10 Minutes

Ingredients:

- ½ cup avocado oil
- 1 ½ cup almond flour
- ½ cup sugar
- 2 tsp almond extract

Directions:

1. Add the almond flour and sugar and pulse to your food processor until the mixture is ground. Add the almond extract and pulse until combined. With the processor running, stream in oil until the mixture starts to form a large ball. Turn off the food processor. With hands, form the marzipan into six 1-inch diameter balls. Press to hold the mixture together. Store in an airtight container in the refrigerator for up to 14 days.

Nutrition Info:

- Per Serving: Calories: 157;Fat: 17g;Protein: 2g;Carbs: 0g.

Simple Apple Compote

Servings:4 | Cooking Time: 10 Minutes

Ingredients:

- 6 apples, peeled, cored, and chopped
- ¼ cup raw honey
- 1 teaspoon ground cinnamon
- ¼ cup apple juice
- Sea salt, to taste

Directions:

1. Put all the ingredients in a stockpot. Stir to mix well, then cook over medium-high heat for 10 minutes or until the apples are glazed by honey and lightly saucy. Stir constantly.
2. Serve immediately.

Nutrition Info:

- Per Serving: Calories: 246;Fat: 0.9g;Protein: 1.2g;Carbs: 66.3g.

Charred Asparagus

Servings:4 | Cooking Time:25 Minutes

Ingredients:

- 2 tbsp olive oil
- 1 lb asparagus, trimmed
- 4 tbsp Grana Padano, grated
- ½ tsp garlic powder
- Salt to taste
- 2 tbsp parsley, chopped

Directions:

1. Preheat the grill to high. Season the asparagus with salt and garlic powder and coat with olive oil. Grill the asparagus for 10 minutes, turning often until lightly charred and tender. Sprinkle with cheese and parsley and serve.

Nutrition Info:

- Per Serving: Calories: 105;Fat: 8g;Protein: 4.3g;Carbs: 4.7g.

Easy Mixed Berry Crisp

Servings:2 | Cooking Time: 30 Minutes

Ingredients:

- 1½ cups frozen mixed berries, thawed
- 1 tablespoon coconut sugar
- 1 tablespoon almond butter
- ¼ cup oats
- ¼ cup pecans

Directions:

1. Preheat the oven to 350°F.
2. Divide the mixed berries between 2 ramekins
3. Place the coconut sugar, almond butter, oats, and pecans in a food processor, and pulse a few times, until the mixture resembles damp sand.
4. Divide the crumble topping over the mixed berries.
5. Put the ramekins on a sheet pan and bake for 30 minutes, or until the top is golden and the berries are bubbling.
6. Serve warm.

Nutrition Info:

- Per Serving: Calories: 268;Fat: 17.0g;Protein: 4.1g;Carbs: 26.8g.

Speedy Granita

Servings:4 | Cooking Time:10 Min + Freezing Time

Ingredients:

- ¼ cup sugar
- 1 cup fresh strawberries
- 1 cup fresh raspberries
- 1 cup chopped fresh kiwi
- 1 tsp lemon juice

Directions:

1. Bring 1 cup water to a boil in a small saucepan over high heat. Add the sugar and stir well until dissolved. Remove the pan from the heat, add the fruit and lemon juice, and cool to room temperature. Once cooled, puree the fruit in a blender until smooth. Pour the puree into a shallow glass baking dish and place in the freezer for 1 hour. Stir with a fork and freeze for 30 minutes, then repeat. Serve and enjoy!

Nutrition Info:

- Per Serving: Calories: 153;Fat: 0.2g;Protein: 1.6g;Carbs: 39g.

Berry Sorbet

Servings:4 | Cooking Time:10 Min + Freezing Time

Ingredients:

- 1 tsp lemon juice
- ¼ cup honey
- 1 cup fresh strawberries
- 1 cup fresh raspberries
- 1 cup fresh blueberries

Directions:

1. Bring 1 cup of water to a boil in a pot over high heat. Stir in honey until dissolved. Remove from the heat and mix in berries and lemon juice; let cool.
2. Once cooled, add the mixture to a food processor and pulse until smooth. Transfer to a shallow glass and freeze for 1 hour. Stir with a fork and freeze for 30 more minutes. Repeat a couple of times. Serve in dessert dishes.

Nutrition Info:

- Per Serving: Calories: 115;Fat: 1g;Protein: 1g;Carbs: 29g.

Fancy Baileys Ice Coffee

Servings:4 | Cooking Time:5 Min + Chilling Time

Ingredients:

- 1 cup espresso
- 2 cups milk
- 4 tbsp Baileys
- ½ tsp ground cinnamon
- ½ tsp vanilla extract
- Ice cubes

Directions:

1. Fill four glasses with ice cubes. Mix milk, cinnamon, and vanilla in a food processor until nice and frothy. Pour into the glasses. Combine the Baileys with the espresso and mix well. Pour ¼ of the espresso mixture over the milk and serve.

Nutrition Info:

- Per Serving: Calories: 100;Fat: 5g;Protein: 4g;Carbs: 8g.

Apple And Berries Ambrosia

Servings:4 | Cooking Time: 0 Minutes

Ingredients:

- 2 cups unsweetened coconut milk, chilled
- 2 tablespoons raw honey
- 1 apple, peeled, cored, and chopped
- 2 cups fresh raspberries
- 2 cups fresh blueberries

Directions:

1. Spoon the chilled milk in a large bowl, then mix in the honey. Stir to mix well.
2. Then mix in the remaining ingredients. Stir to coat the fruits well and serve immediately.

Nutrition Info:

- Per Serving: Calories: 386;Fat: 21.1g;Protein: 4.2g;Carbs: 45.9g.

Pesto & Egg Avocado Boats

Servings:2 | Cooking Time:15 Minutes

Ingredients:

- 1 halved avocado, pitted
- 2 large eggs
- Salt and black pepper to taste
- 2 tbsp jarred pesto
- 2 sundried tomatoes, chopped

Directions:

1. Preheat oven to 420 °F. Scoop out the middle of each avocado half. Arrange them on a baking sheet, cut-side up. Crack an egg into each avocado half and season to taste. Bake until the eggs are set and cooked to your desired level of doneness, 10-12 minutes. Remove from the oven and top with pesto and sundried tomatoes. Serve and enjoy!

Nutrition Info:

- Per Serving: Calories: 302;Fat: 26g;Protein: 8g;Carbs: 10g.

Charred Maple Pineapple

Servings:4 | Cooking Time:10 Minutes

Ingredients:

- 1 pineapple, peeled and cut into wedges
- 1 tbsp maple syrup
- ½ tsp ground cinnamon

Directions:

1. Preheat a grill pan over high heat. Place the fruit in a bowl and drizzle with maple syrup; sprinkle with ground cinnamon. Grill for about 7-8 minutes, turning occasionally until the fruit chars slightly. Serve.

Nutrition Info:

- Per Serving: Calories: 130;Fat: 0g;Protein: 1g;Carbs: 32g.

Honey & Spice Roasted Almonds

Servings:4 | Cooking Time:15 Minutes

Ingredients:

- 2 tbsp olive oil
- 3 cups almonds
- 1 tbsp curry powder
- ¼ cup honey
- 1 tsp salt

Directions:

1. Preheat oven to 260 °F. Coat almonds with olive oil, curry powder, and salt in a bowl; mix well. Arrange on a lined with aluminum foil sheet and bake for 15 minutes. Remove from the oven and let cool for 10 minutes. Drizzle with honey and let cool at room temperature. Enjoy!

Nutrition Info:

- Per Serving: Calories: 134;Fat: 8g;Protein: 1g;Carbs: 18g.

Balsamic Strawberry Caprese Skewers

Servings:6 | Cooking Time:15 Min + Cooling Time

Ingredients:

- 1 tbsp olive oil
- 1 cup balsamic vinegar
- 24 whole, hulled strawberries
- 24 basil leaves, halved
- 12 fresh mozzarella balls

Directions:

1. Pour the balsamic vinegar into a small saucepan and simmer for 10 minutes or until it's reduced by half and is thick enough to coat the back of a spoon. Set aside to cool completely. Thread the strawberries onto wooden skewers, followed by basil leaves folded in half and mozzarella balls. Drizzle with balsamic glaze and olive oil and serve.

Nutrition Info:

- Per Serving: Calories: 206;Fat: 10g;Protein: 10g;Carbs: 17g.

Dates Stuffed With Mascarpone & Almonds

Servings:6 | Cooking Time:10 Minutes

Ingredients:

- 20 blanched almonds
- 8 oz mascarpone cheese
- 20 Medjool dates
- 2 tbsp honey

Directions:

1. Using a knife, cut one side of the date lengthwise from the stem to the bottom. Gently remove the stone and replace it with a blanched almond. Spoon the cheese into a piping bag. Squeeze a generous amount of the cheese into each date. Set the dates on a serving plate and drizzle with honey. Serve immediately or chill in the fridge.

Nutrition Info:

- Per Serving: Calories: 253;Fat: 15g;Protein: 2g;Carbs: 31g.

Strawberry Parfait

Servings:2 | Cooking Time:10 Minutes

Ingredients:

- ¾ cup Greek yogurt
- 1 tbsp cocoa powder
- ¼ cup strawberries, chopped
- 5 drops vanilla stevia

Directions:

1. Combine cocoa powder, strawberries, yogurt, and stevia in a bowl. Serve immediately.

Nutrition Info:

- Per Serving: Calories: 210;Fat: 9g;Protein: 5g;Carbs: 8g.

Minty Yogurt & Banana Cups

Servings:2 | Cooking Time:5 Minutes

Ingredients:
- 2 bananas, sliced
- 2 cups Greek yogurt
- 1 tsp cinnamon
- 3 tbsp honey
- 2 tbsp mint leaves, chopped

Directions:

1. Divide the yogurt between 2 cups and top with banana slices, cinnamon, honey, and mint. Serve immediately.

Nutrition Info:
- Per Serving: Calories: 355;Fat: 4.2g;Protein: 22g;Carbs: 61g.

Crispy Sesame Cookies

Servings:14 | Cooking Time: 8 To 10 Minutes

Ingredients:
- 1 cup hulled sesame seeds
- 1 cup sugar
- 8 tablespoons almond butter
- 2 large eggs
- 1¼ cups flour

Directions:

1. Preheat the oven to 350ºF.
2. Toast the sesame seeds on a baking sheet for 3 minutes. Set aside and let cool.
3. Using a mixer, whisk together the sugar and butter. Add the eggs one at a time until well blended. Add the flour and toasted sesame seeds and mix until well blended.
4. Drop spoonfuls of cookie dough onto a baking sheet and form them into round balls, about 1-inch in diameter, similar to a walnut.
5. Put in the oven and bake for 5 to 7 minutes, or until golden brown.
6. Let the cookies cool for 5 minutes before serving.

Nutrition Info:
- Per Serving: Calories: 218;Fat: 12.0g;Protein: 4.0g;Carbs: 25.0g.

Chocolate, Almond, And Cherry Clusters

Servings:10 | Cooking Time: 3 Minutes

Ingredients:

- 1 cup dark chocolate, chopped
- 1 tablespoon coconut oil
- ½ cup dried cherries
- 1 cup roasted salted almonds

Directions:

1. Line a baking sheet with parchment paper.
2. Melt the chocolate and coconut oil in a saucepan for 3 minutes. Stir constantly.
3. Turn off the heat and mix in the cherries and almonds.
4. Drop the mixture on the baking sheet with a spoon. Place the sheet in the refrigerator and chill for at least 1 hour or until firm.
5. Serve chilled.

Nutrition Info:

- Per Serving: Calories: 197;Fat: 13.2g;Protein: 4.1g;Carbs: 17.8g.

Shallot & Kale Spread

Servings:4 | Cooking Time:10 Minutes

Ingredients:

- 2 shallots, chopped
- 1 lb kale, roughly chopped
- 2 tbsp mint, chopped
- ¾ cup cream cheese, soft
- Salt and black pepper to taste

Directions:

1. In a food processor, blend kale, shallots, mint, cream cheese, salt, and pepper until smooth. Serve.

Nutrition Info:

- Per Serving: Calories: 210;Fat: 12g;Protein: 6g;Carbs: 5g.

Pesto Arugula Dip

Servings:4 | Cooking Time:5 Minutes

Ingredients:

- 1 cup arugula, chopped
- 3 tbsp basil pesto
- 1 cup cream cheese, soft
- Salt and black pepper to taste
- 1 cup heavy cream
- 1 tbsp chives, chopped

Directions:

1. Combine arugula, basil pesto, salt, pepper, and heavy cream in a blender and pulse until smooth. Transfer to a bowl and mix in cream cheese. Serve topped with chives.

Nutrition Info:

- Per Serving: Calories: 240;Fat: 15g;Protein: 6g;Carbs: 7g.

Choco-tahini Glazed Apple Chips

Servings:2 | Cooking Time:10 Minutes

Ingredients:

- 1 tbsp roasted, salted sunflower seeds
- 2 tbsp tahini
- 1 tbsp honey
- 1 tbsp cocoa powder
- 2 apples, thinly sliced

Directions:

1. Mix the tahini, honey, and cocoa powder in a small bowl. Add 1-2 tbsp of warm water and stir until thin enough to drizzle. Lay the apple chips out on a plate and drizzle them with the chocolate tahini sauce. Sprinkle sunflower seeds.

Nutrition Info:

- Per Serving: Calories: 261;Fat: 11g;Protein: 5g;Carbs: 43g.

Pomegranate Blueberry Granita

Servings:2 | Cooking Time:15 Min + Freezing Time

Ingredients:

- 1 cup blueberries
- 1 cup pomegranate juice
- ¼ cup sugar
- ¼ tsp lemon zest

Directions:

1. Place the blueberries, lemon zest, and pomegranate juice in a saucepan over medium heat and bring to a boil. Simmer for 5 minutes or until the blueberries start to break down. Stir the sugar in ¼ cup of water until the sugar is dissolved. Place the blueberry mixture and the sugar water in your blender and blitz for 1 minute or until the fruit is puréed.
2. Pour the mixture into a baking pan. The liquid should come about ½ inch up the sides. Let the mixture cool for 30 minutes, and then put it into the freezer. Every 30 minutes for the next 2 hours, scrape the granita with a fork to keep it from freezing solid. Serve it after 2 hours, or store it in a covered container in the freezer.

Nutrition Info:

- Per Serving: Calories: 214;Fat: 0g;Protein: 1g;Carbs: 54g.

Prawn & Cucumber Bites

Servings:4 | Cooking Time:5 Minutes

Ingredients:

- 1 lb prawns, cooked and chopped
- 1 cucumber, cubed
- 2 tbsp cream cheese
- Salt and black pepper to taste
- 12 whole-grain crackers

Directions:

1. Combine cucumber, prawns, cream cheese, salt, and pepper in a bowl. Place crackers on a plate and top them with the prawn mixture. Serve right away.

Nutrition Info:

- Per Serving: Calories: 160;Fat: 9g;Protein: 18g;Carbs: 12g.

Crispy Kale Chips

Servings:4 | Cooking Time:15 Minutes

Ingredients:

- 2 tbsp olive oil
- 2 heads curly leaf kale
- Sea salt to taste

Directions:

1. Tear the kale into bite-sized pieces. Toss with the olive oil, and lay on a baking sheet in a single layer. Sprinkle with a pinch of sea salt. Bake for 10 to 15 minutes until crispy. Serve or store in an airtight container.

Nutrition Info:

- Per Serving: Calories: 102;Fat: 4g;Protein: 6g;Carbs: 14g.

Cardamom Apple Slices

Servings:2 | Cooking Time:30 Minutes

Ingredients:

- 1 ½ tsp cardamom
- ½ tsp salt
- 4 peeled, cored apples, sliced
- 2 tbsp honey
- 2 tbsp milk

Directions:

1. Preheat oven to 390 °F. In a bowl, combine apple slices, salt, and ½ tsp of cardamom. Arrange them on a greased baking dish and cook for 20 minutes. Remove to a serving plate.
2. In the meantime, place milk, honey, and remaining cardamom in a pot over medium heat. Cook until simmer. Pour the sauce over the apples and serve immediately.

Nutrition Info:

- Per Serving: Calories: 287;Fat: 3g;Protein: 2g;Carbs: 69g.

Crispy Potato Chips

Servings:4 | Cooking Time:40 Minutes

Ingredients:
- 2 tbsp olive oil
- 4 potatoes, cut into wedges
- 2 tbsp grated Parmesan cheese
- Salt and black pepper to taste

Directions:

1. Preheat the oven to 340 °F. In a bowl, combine the potatoes, olive oil, salt, and black pepper. Spread on a lined baking sheet and bake for 40 minutes until the edges are browned. Serve sprinkled with Parmesan cheese.

Nutrition Info:
- Per Serving: Calories: 359;Fat: 8g;Protein: 9g;Carbs: 66g.

Pecan & Raspberry & Frozen Yogurt Cups

Servings:4 | Cooking Time:10 Minutes

Ingredients:
- 2 cups fresh raspberries
- 4 cups vanilla frozen yogurt
- 1 lime, zested
- ¼ cup chopped praline pecans

Directions:

1. Divide the frozen yogurt into 4 dessert glasses. Top with raspberries, lime zest, and pecans. Serve immediately.

Nutrition Info:
- Per Serving: Calories: 142;Fat: 3.4g;Protein: 3.7g;Carbs: 26g.

Iberian Spread For Sandwiches

Servings:4 | Cooking Time:10 Minutes

Ingredients:
- 16 pimiento stuffed manzanilla olives
- 4 oz roasted pimientos
- 2/3 cup aioli

Directions:

1. Place the olives and roasted pimientos in your food processor. Pulse until a creamier consistency is formed. Transfer to a bowl and mix well with aioli. Serve and enjoy!

Nutrition Info:
- Per Serving: Calories: 325;Fat: 34g;Protein: 0.1g;Carbs: 2g.

Mini Cucumber & Cream Cheese Sandwiches

Servings:4 | Cooking Time:5 Minutes

Ingredients:

- 4 bread slices
- 1 cucumber, sliced
- 2 tbsp cream cheese, soft
- 1 tbsp chives, chopped
- ¼ cup hummus
- Salt and black pepper to taste

Directions:

1. In a bowl, mix hummus, cream cheese, chives, salt, and pepper until well combined. Spread the mixture onto bread slices. Top with cucumber and cut each sandwich into three pieces. Serve immediately.

Nutrition Info:

- Per Serving: Calories: 190;Fat: 13g;Protein: 9g;Carbs: 5g.

Skillet Pesto Pizza

Servings:2 | Cooking Time:10 Minutes

Ingredients:

- 1 tbsp butter
- 2 pieces of focaccia bread
- 2 tbsp pesto
- 1 medium tomato, sliced
- 2 large eggs

Directions:

1. Place a large skillet over medium heat. Place the focaccia in the skillet and let it warm for about 4 minutes on both sides until softened and just starting to turn golden. Remove to a platter. Spread 1 tablespoon of the pesto on one side of each slice. Cover with tomato slices. Melt the butter in the skillet over medium heat. Crack in the eggs, keeping them separated, and cook until the whites are no longer translucent and the yolk is cooked to desired doneness. Spoon one egg onto each pizza. Serve and enjoy!

Nutrition Info:

- Per Serving: Calories: 427;Fat: 17g;Protein: 17g;Carbs: 10g.

Sicilian Almond Granita

Servings:4 | Cooking Time:5 Min + Freezing Time

Ingredients:

- 4 small oranges, chopped
- ½ tsp almond extract
- 2 tbsp lemon juice
- 1 cup orange juice
- ¼ cup honey
- Fresh mint leaves for garnish

Directions:

1. In a food processor, mix oranges, orange juice, honey, almond extract, and lemon juice. Pulse until smooth. Pour in a dip dish and freeze for 1 hour. Mix with a fork and freeze for 30 minutes more. Repeat a couple of times. Pour into dessert glasses and garnish with basil leaves. Serve.

Nutrition Info:

- Per Serving: Calories: 145;Fat: 0g;Protein: 1.5g;Carbs: 36g.

Glazed Pears With Hazelnuts

Servings:4 | Cooking Time: 20 Minutes

Ingredients:

- 4 pears, peeled, cored, and quartered lengthwise
- 1 cup apple juice
- 1 tablespoon grated fresh ginger
- ½ cup pure maple syrup
- ¼ cup chopped hazelnuts

Directions:

1. Put the pears in a pot, then pour in the apple juice. Bring to a boil over medium-high heat, then reduce the heat to medium-low. Stir constantly.
2. Cover and simmer for an additional 15 minutes or until the pears are tender.
3. Meanwhile, combine the ginger and maple syrup in a saucepan. Bring to a boil over medium-high heat. Stir frequently. Turn off the heat and transfer the syrup to a small bowl and let sit until ready to use.
4. Transfer the pears in a large serving bowl with a slotted spoon, then top the pears with syrup.
5. Spread the hazelnuts over the pears and serve immediately.

Nutrition Info:

- Per Serving: Calories: 287;Fat: 3.1g;Protein: 2.2g;Carbs: 66.9g.

Fig & Mascarpone Toasts With Pistachios

Servings:6 | Cooking Time:10 Minutes

Ingredients:

- 4 tbsp butter, melted
- 1 French baguette, sliced
- 1 cup Mascarpone cheese
- 1 jar fig jam
- ½ cup crushed pistachios

Directions:

1. Preheat oven to 350 °F. Arrange the sliced bread on a greased baking sheet and brush each slice with melted butter.
2. Toast the bread for 5-7 minutes until golden brown. Let the bread cool slightly. Spread about a teaspoon of the mascarpone cheese on each piece of bread. Top with fig jam and pistachios.

Nutrition Info:

- Per Serving: Calories: 445;Fat: 24g;Protein: 3g;Carbs: 48g.

Italian Submarine-style Sandwiches

Servings:4 | Cooking Time:35 Minutes

Ingredients:

- ½ lb sliced deli ham
- ½ lb sliced deli turkey
- 1 Italian loaf bread, unsliced
- 1/3 cup honey mustard
- ½ lb sliced mozzarella cheese

Directions:

1. Preheat oven to 400 °F. Cut the bread horizontally in half. Spread the honey mustard over the bottom half. Layer ham, turkey, and mozzarella cheese over, then top with the remaining bread half. Wrap the sandwich in foil and bake for 20 minutes or until the bread is toasted. Open the foil and bake for 5 minutes or until the top is crisp. Serve sliced.

Nutrition Info:

- Per Serving: Calories: 704;Fat: 17g;Protein: 50g;Carbs: 85g.

Garlic-yogurt Dip With Walnuts

Servings:4 | Cooking Time:5 Minutes

Ingredients:

- 2 cups Greek yogurt
- 3 garlic cloves, minced
- ¼ cup dill, chopped
- 1 green onion, chopped
- ¼ cup walnuts, chopped
- Salt and black pepper to taste

Directions:

1. Combine garlic, yogurt, dill, walnuts, salt, and pepper in a bowl. Serve topped with green onion.

Nutrition Info:

- Per Serving: Calories: 210;Fat: 7g;Protein: 9g;Carbs: 16g.

Crunchy Almond Cookies

Servings:4 | Cooking Time: 5 To 7 Minutes

Ingredients:
- ½ cup sugar
- 8 tablespoons almond butter
- 1 large egg
- 1½ cups all-purpose flour
- 1 cup ground almonds

Directions:

1. Preheat the oven to 375°F. Line a baking sheet with parchment paper.
2. Using a mixer, whisk together the sugar and butter. Add the egg and mix until combined. Alternately add the flour and ground almonds, ½ cup at a time, while the mixer is on slow.
3. Drop 1 tablespoon of the dough on the prepared baking sheet, keeping the cookies at least 2 inches apart.
4. Put the baking sheet in the oven and bake for about 5 to 7 minutes, or until the cookies start to turn brown around the edges.
5. Let cool for 5 minutes before serving.

Nutrition Info:
- Per Serving: Calories: 604;Fat: 36.0g;Protein: 11.0g;Carbs: 63.0g.

Grilled Stone Fruit With Honey

Servings:2 | Cooking Time: 6 Minutes

Ingredients:
- 3 apricots, halved and pitted
- 2 plums, halved and pitted
- 2 peaches, halved and pitted
- ½ cup low-fat ricotta cheese
- 2 tablespoons honey
- Cooking spray

Directions:

1. Preheat the grill to medium heat. Spray the grill grates with cooking spray.
2. Arrange the fruit, cut side down, on the grill, and cook for 2 to 3 minutes per side, or until lightly charred and softened.
3. Serve warm with a sprinkle of cheese and a drizzle of honey.

Nutrition Info:
- Per Serving: Calories: 298;Fat: 7.8g;Protein: 11.9g;Carbs: 45.2g.

Goat Cheese Dip With Scallions & Lemon

Servings:4 | Cooking Time:10 Minutes

Ingredients:

- 2 tbsp extra virgin olive oil
- 2 oz goat cheese, crumbled
- ¾ cup sour cream
- 2 tbsp scallions, chopped
- 1 tbsp lemon juice
- Salt and black pepper to taste

Directions:

1. Combine goat cheese, sour cream, scallions, lemon juice, salt, pepper, and olive oil in a bowl and transfer to the fridge for 10 minutes before serving.

Nutrition Info:

- Per Serving: Calories: 230;Fat: 12g;Protein: 6g;Carbs: 9g.

Savory Cauliflower Steaks

Servings:4 | Cooking Time:35 Minutes

Ingredients:

- 1 head cauliflower, cut into steaks
- 2 tbsp olive oil
- Salt and paprika to taste

Directions:

1. Preheat oven to 360 °F.Line a baking sheet with aluminum foil. Rub each cauliflower steak with olive oil, salt, and paprika. Arrange on the baking sheet and bake for 10-15 minutes, flip, and bake for another 15 minutes until crispy.

Nutrition Info:

- Per Serving: Calories: 78;Fat: 7g;Protein: 1g;Carbs: 4g.

Thyme Lentil Spread

Servings:6 | Cooking Time:10 Minutes

Ingredients:

- 3 tbsp olive oil
- 1 garlic clove, minced
- 1 cup split red lentils, rinsed
- ½ tsp dried thyme
- 1 tbsp balsamic vinegar
- Salt and black pepper to taste

Directions:

1. Bring to a boil salted water in a pot over medium heat. Add in the lentils and cook for 15 minutes until cooked through. Drain and set aside to cool. In a food processor, place the lentils, garlic, thyme, vinegar, salt, and pepper. Gradually add olive oil while blending until smooth. Serve.

Nutrition Info:

- Per Serving: Calories: 295;Fat: 10g;Protein: 10g;Carbs: 16g.

Baked Beet Fries With Feta Cheese

Servings:4 | Cooking Time:40 Minutes

Ingredients:
- 1 cup olive oil
- 1 cup feta cheese, crumbled
- 2 beets, sliced
- Salt and black pepper to taste
- 1/3 cup balsamic vinegar

Directions:

1. Preheat the oven to 340 °F. Line a baking sheet with parchment paper. Arrange beet slices, salt, pepper, vinegar, and olive oil on the sheet and toss to combine. Bake for 30 minutes. Serve topped with feta cheese.

Nutrition Info:
- Per Serving: Calories: 210;Fat: 6g;Protein: 4g;Carbs: 9g.

Salt & Pepper Toasted Walnuts

Servings:6 | Cooking Time:20 Minutes

Ingredients:
- 2 tbsp olive oil
- 4 cups walnut halves
- Sea salt flakes to taste
- Black pepper to taste

Directions:

1. Preheat the oven to 250 °F. In a bowl, toss the walnuts with olive oil, salt, and pepper to coat. Spread out the walnuts on a parchment-lined baking sheet. Toast for 10-15 minutes. Remove from the oven and allow to cool completely. Serve.

Nutrition Info:
- Per Serving: Calories: 193;Fat: 2g;Protein: 8g;Carbs: 23g.

30 Day Meal Plan

	Breakfast	Lunch	Dinner
Day 1	Eggs Florentine With Pancetta	Anchovy Spread With Avocado	Asparagus & Red Onion Side Dish
Day 2	Easy Buckwheat Porridge	Pancetta-wrapped Scallops	Cherry, Plum, Artichoke, And Cheese Board
Day 3	Pecan & Peach Parfait	Lemony Sea Bass	Homemade Herbes De Provence Spice
Day 4	Cinnamon Oatmeal With Dried Cranberries	Parsley Tomato Tilapia	Orange-honey Glazed Carrots
Day 5	Creamy Vanilla Oatmeal	Creamy Beef Stew	Creamy Tomato Hummus Soup
Day 6	Cheese & Mushroom Muffins	Peppercorn-seared Tuna Steaks	Easy Roasted Cauliflower
Day 7	Avocado Toast With Goat Cheese	Greek-style Lamb Burgers	Zesty Asparagus Salad
Day 8	Cream Peach Smoothie	Balsamic Asparagus & Salmon Roast	Greek Chicken, Tomato, And Olive Salad
Day 9	Raspberry-yogurt Smoothie	Original Meatballs	Balsamic Carrots With Feta Cheese
Day 10	Mango-yogurt Smoothie	Herby Tuna Gratin	Tasty Cucumber & Couscous Salad
Day 11	Chili & Cheese Frittata	Rosemary Pork Loin With Green Onions	Parsley Carrot & Cabbage Salad
Day 12	Maple Peach Smoothie	Salmon Packets	Simple Zoodles
Day 13	One-pan Tomato-basil Eggs	Pork Tenderloin With Caraway Seeds	Pea & Carrot Noodles
Day 14	Lime Watermelon Yogurt Smoothie	Creamy Trout Spread	Balsamic Cherry Tomatoes
Day 15	Maple-vanilla Yogurt With Walnuts	Grilled Beef With Mint-jalapeño Vinaigrette	Cauliflower Rice Risotto With Mushrooms

	Breakfast	**Lunch**	**Dinner**
Day 16	Tomato And Egg Breakfast Pizza	Baked Anchovies With Chili-garlic Topping	Wilted Dandelion Greens With Sweet Onion
Day 17	Oven-baked Mozzarella Cheese Cups	Crispy Pesto Chicken	Grilled Za´atar Zucchini Rounds
Day 18	Hot Zucchini & Egg Nests	Balsamic-honey Glazed Salmon	Garlicky Broccoli Rabe
Day 19	Easy Zucchini & Egg Stuffed Tomatoes	Pork Millet With Chestnuts	Sautéed Mushrooms With Garlic & Parsley
Day 20	Basic Tortilla De Patatas	Grilled Lemon Pesto Salmon	Spicy Potato Wedges
Day 21	Apple & Date Smoothie	Chicken Caprese	Baby Kale And Cabbage Salad
Day 22	Honey & Feta Frozen Yogurt	Glazed Broiled Salmon	Roasted Asparagus With Hazelnuts
Day 23	Simple Mushroom Omelet	Tomato Walnut Chicken	Minty Broccoli & Walnuts
Day 24	Strawberry Basil Mascarpone Toast	Rosemary Wine Poached Haddock	Parmesan Stuffed Zucchini Boats
Day 25	5-ingredient Quinoa Breakfast Bowls	Baked Garlicky Pork Chops	Tradicional Matchuba Green Beans
Day 26	Berry & Cheese Omelet	Crunchy Pollock Fillets	Stuffed Portobello Mushrooms With Spinach
Day 27	Baked Eggs In Avocado	Peach Pork Chops	Garlic-butter Asparagus With Parmesan
Day 28	Maple Berry & Walnut Oatmeal	Simple Fried Cod Fillets	Simple Broccoli With Yogurt Sauce
Day 29	Berry-yogurt Smoothie	Baked Salmon With Basil And Tomato	Baked Honey Acorn Squash
Day 30	Za'atar Pizza	Easy Grilled Pork Chops	Quick Steamed Broccoli

Appendix : Recipes Index

5-ingredient Quinoa Breakfast Bowls 18
5-ingredient Zucchini Fritters 56
5-minute Avocado Spread 80

A

Anchovy & Spinach Sandwiches 21
Anchovy Spread With Avocado 37
Apple & Date Smoothie 16
Apple And Berries Ambrosia 83
Arugula, Watermelon, And Feta Salad 68
Asparagus & Red Onion Side Dish 67
Avocado Toast With Goat Cheese 12

B

Baby Kale And Cabbage Salad 53
Baked Anchovies With Chili-garlic Topping 39
Baked Beet Fries With Feta Cheese 96
Baked Eggs In Avocado 19
Baked Garlicky Pork Chops 31
Baked Haddock With Rosemary Gremolata 45
Baked Honey Acorn Squash 49
Baked Lemon Salmon 45
Baked Salmon With Basil And Tomato 42
Balsamic Asparagus & Salmon Roast 38
Balsamic Carrots With Feta Cheese 61
Balsamic Cherry Tomatoes 57
Balsamic Potato Salad With Capers 73
Balsamic Roasted Mushrooms 69
Balsamic Strawberry Caprese Skewers 85
Balsamic Watermelon & Feta Salad 68
Balsamic-honey Glazed Salmon 39
Basic Tortilla De Patatas 16
Berry & Cheese Omelet 18
Berry Sorbet 83
Berry-yogurt Smoothie 20
Broccoli And Carrot Pasta Salad 27

C

Cantaloupe & Watermelon Balls 77
Cardamom Apple Slices 89
Cauliflower Rice Risotto With Mushrooms 57
Charred Asparagus 81
Charred Maple Pineapple 84
Cheese & Mushroom Muffins 11
Cheesy Peach And Walnut Salad 70
Cheesy Roasted Broccolini 71
Cherry, Plum, Artichoke, And Cheese Board 66
Chicken Caprese 31
Chili & Cheese Frittata 13
Chive Ricotta Spread 78
Chocolate, Almond, And Cherry Clusters 87
Choco-tahini Glazed Apple Chips 88
Cinnamon Oatmeal With Dried Cranberries 10
Classic Aioli 72
Classic Potato Salad With Green Onions 68
Coconut Blueberries With Brown Rice 77
Crab Stuffed Celery Sticks 42
Cranberry And Almond Quinoa 25
Cream Peach Smoothie 12
Creamy Beef Stew 34
Creamy Tomato Hummus Soup 64
Creamy Trout Spread 39
Creamy Vanilla Oatmeal 11
Crispy Kale Chips 89
Crispy Pesto Chicken 32
Crispy Potato Chips 90
Crispy Sesame Cookies 86
Crispy Sole Fillets 44
Crunchy Almond Cookies 94
Crunchy Pollock Fillets 42
Cucumber Salad With Goat Cheese 74

D

Dark Chocolate Barks 78
Dates Stuffed With Mascarpone & Almonds 85
Dilly Haddock In Tomato Sauce 36

E

Easy Buckwheat Porridge   9
Easy Grilled Pork Chops   30
Easy Mixed Berry Crisp   82
Easy Roasted Cauliflower   64
Easy Zucchini & Egg Stuffed Tomatoes   16
Effortless Bell Pepper Salad   72
Eggs Florentine With Pancetta   9

F

Fancy Baileys Ice Coffee   83
Fig & Mascarpone Toasts With Pistachios   93
Fruit And Nut Chocolate Bark   80
Fruit Skewers With Vanilla Labneh   79

G

Garlic Herb Butter   63
Garlic Wilted Greens   74
Garlic-butter Asparagus With Parmesan   50
Garlicky Broccoli Rabe   55
Garlic-yogurt Dip With Walnuts   93
Glazed Broiled Salmon   41
Glazed Pears With Hazelnuts   92
Goat Cheese Dip With Scallions & Lemon   95
Granola & Berry Parfait   21
Greek Chicken, Tomato, And Olive Salad   61
Greek Tahini Sauce   67
Greek-style Lamb Burgers   34
Green Beans With Tahini-lemon Sauce   62
Grilled Beef With Mint-jalapeño Vinaigrette   33
Grilled Lemon Pesto Salmon   40
Grilled Pesto Halloumi Cheese   76
Grilled Stone Fruit With Honey   94
Grilled Za´atar Zucchini Rounds   56

H

Hazelnut Crusted Sea Bass   46
Herby Tuna Gratin   38
Herby Yogurt Sauce   65
Homemade Herbes De Provence Spice   66
Honey & Feta Frozen Yogurt   17
Honey & Spice Roasted Almonds   84
Hot Zucchini & Egg Nests   15

Hummus & Tomato Stuffed Cucumbers   78

I

Iberian Spread For Sandwiches   90
Instant Pot Poached Salmon   43
Italian Submarine-style Sandwiches   93

K

Kid´s Marzipan Balls   81

L

Lemon Couscous With Broccoli   26
Lemon-basil Spaghetti   26
Lemon-garlic Sea Bass   44
Lemony Sea Bass   36
Lemony Yogurt Sauce   63
Lime Watermelon Yogurt Smoothie   14

M

Mango-yogurt Smoothie   13
Maple Berry & Walnut Oatmeal   19
Maple Peach Smoothie   13
Maple-vanilla Yogurt With Walnuts   14
Mascarpone Sweet Potato Mash   70
Mediterranean Tomato Hummus Soup   72
Mini Cucumber & Cream Cheese Sandwiches   91
Mint Brown Rice   27
Mint-watermelon Gelato   76
Minty Broccoli & Walnuts   52
Minty Yogurt & Banana Cups   86

N

North African Grilled Fish Fillets   47

O

Oil–poached Cod   46
One-pan Tomato-basil Eggs   14
One-step Couscous   23
Orange-honey Glazed Carrots   65
Original Meatballs   34

Oven-baked Mozzarella Cheese Cups   15

P

Pancetta-wrapped Scallops   37
Parchment Orange & Dill Salmon   47
Parmesan Polenta   25
Parmesan Stuffed Zucchini Boats   52
Parsley Carrot & Cabbage Salad   60
Parsley Tomato Tilapia   36
Pea & Carrot Noodles   58
Peach Pork Chops   30
Pecan & Peach Parfait   10
Pecan & Raspberry & Frozen Yogurt Cups   90
Pecorino Zucchini Strips   73
Peppercorn-seared Tuna Steaks   37
Pesto & Egg Avocado Boats   84
Pesto Arugula Dip   87
Pomegranate Blueberry Granita   88
Pork Millet With Chestnuts   32
Pork Tenderloin With Caraway Seeds   33
Prawn & Cucumber Bites   89

Q

Quick Pesto Pasta   28
Quick Steamed Broccoli   49
Quick Za´atar Spice   69
Quinoa With Baby Potatoes And Broccoli   23

R

Raspberry & Nut Quinoa   28
Raspberry-yogurt Smoothie   12
Roasted Asparagus With Hazelnuts   53
Roasted Cherry Tomato & Fennel   67
Rosemary Garlic Infused Olive Oil   70
Rosemary Pork Loin With Green Onions   33
Rosemary Wine Poached Haddock   41

S

Salmon In Thyme Tomato Sauce   40
Salmon Packets   38
Salt & Pepper Toasted Walnuts   96
Sautéed Mushrooms With Garlic & Parsley   54
Savory Cauliflower Steaks   95

Shallot & Kale Spread   87
Sicilian Almond Granita   92
Simple Apple Compote   81
Simple Broccoli With Yogurt Sauce   50
Simple Fried Cod Fillets   43
Simple Mushroom Omelet   17
Simple Tahini Sauce   66
Simple Zoodles   58
Skillet Pesto Pizza   91
Spaghetti With Pine Nuts And Cheese   24
Speedy Granita   82
Spicy Potato Wedges   54
Spinach & Bell Pepper Salad   69
Spinach & Cherry Tomato Salad   73
Strawberries With Balsamic Vinegar   79
Strawberry Basil Mascarpone Toast   17
Strawberry Parfait   85
Stuffed Portobello Mushrooms With Spinach   51
Swiss Chard Couscous With Feta Cheese   24

T

Tasty Cucumber & Couscous Salad   60
Thyme Lentil Spread   95
Tomato And Egg Breakfast Pizza   15
Tomato Walnut Chicken   31
Tradicional Matchuba Green Beans   51
Traditional Tuscan Scallops   44

W

Warm Kale Salad With Red Bell Pepper   71
Wilted Dandelion Greens With Sweet Onion   55
Wrapped Pears In Prosciutto   79

Z

Za'atar Pizza   20
Zesty Asparagus Salad   62

Printed in Great Britain
by Amazon

28199966R00057